My Light Body Speaks and Revealing Secrets of Heaven

My Light Body Speaks and Revealing Secrets of Heaven

Automatic Writing

Linda Prior

BALBOA PRESS
A DIVISION OF HAY HOUSE

Copyright © 2015 Linda Prior.

All rights reserved. No part of this book may be used or reproduced by any means, graphic, electronic, or mechanical, including photocopying, recording, taping or by any information storage retrieval system without the written permission of the publisher except in the case of brief quotations embodied in critical articles and reviews.

Balboa Press books may be ordered through booksellers or by contacting:

Balboa Press
A Division of Hay House
1663 Liberty Drive
Bloomington, IN 47403
www.balboapress.com
1 (877) 407-4847

Because of the dynamic nature of the Internet, any web addresses or links contained in this book may have changed since publication and may no longer be valid. The views expressed in this work are solely those of the author and do not necessarily reflect the views of the publisher, and the publisher hereby disclaims any responsibility for them.

The author of this book does not dispense medical advice or prescribe the use of any technique as a form of treatment for physical, emotional, or medical problems without the advice of a physician, either directly or indirectly. The intent of the author is only to offer information of a general nature to help you in your quest for emotional and spiritual well-being. In the event you use any of the information in this book for yourself, which is your constitutional right, the author and the publisher assume no responsibility for your actions.

Any people depicted in stock imagery provided by Thinkstock are models, and such images are being used for illustrative purposes only. Certain stock imagery © Thinkstock.

Print information available on the last page.

ISBN: 978-1-5043-2805-0 (sc)
ISBN: 978-1-5043-2807-4 (hc)
ISBN: 978-1-5043-2806-7 (e)

Library of Congress Control Number: 2015902393

Balboa Press rev. date: 04/28/2015

Table of Contents

Chapter One 1
Chapter Two 11
Chapter Three 22
Chapter Four 37
Chapter Five 47
Chapter Six 58
Chapter Seven 74
Chapter Eight 84
Chapter Nine 92

Chapter One

As a Light Body to the instrument who is typing this book, I want to introduce myself. My name is Adethia. Over a hundred thousand years old, I am an Angel from the angelic kingdom. Whether one is a Cosmic Being, an Angel, or a BEING from other universes, that individual is a Light Body who can serve and help mankind, or the humans, on earth. We Light Bodies do not have to match souls as other species do. Whether the instrument is a Cosmic Being, a BEING, or an Angel, all Light Bodies can serve mankind in any capacity.

    Before I begin to tell the reader what Light Bodies do to help mankind? I want to explain to the reader that the human body is made up of other bodies that help the function of the human and spiritual body upon this earth navigate to specific areas of growth that the soul desires for that particular individual soul to grow. The I am Presence, the Light Body and the Spiritual Body, the Causal body are all separate parts of the human being. The soul lives in the Causal body and leads the other bodies towards the enrichment of Godliness. All experiences that one has encountered upon the earth are for wisdom and growth of that soul. When the human body lays down to sleep the Spiritual body can leave the earth body and do other spiritual work to help mankind. There are many times that many individuals come up to the Karmic board in their spiritual body and plead their case about their life that they want changed on earth. So as the reader begins to understand about their Light Body that it's separate from the human body, but attached to them to help them navigate through life and all its twists and turns that one human being encounters upon earth. We will have examples of souls and how they functioned on earth; their shortcomings, failures and the reasons why they failed a life upon earth. We will also have stories of souls that the author doesn't know showing the reader what not to do or what to do to incorporate into their behavior to succeed in life upon earth. We will take you through the process of the Octaves and what we have been encountering for the last 5 years or since 2010 with the war of good and evil. We will introduce to the reader the Queen of Queens which no one has ever heard of before. And, we will remind the reader to be kind, always have respect for those upon this earth that cross your pathway during your lifetime.

After a human dies on earth, that person's soul leads him or her to the Octaves, which is where all souls that come from the human kingdom live. The universe we inhabit is the only universe where the human species lives. When humans make the ascension (which I will explain later in the book), they become ascended masters for one year, after which time we call them Cosmic Beings. The Octaves serve many purposes. For one, they help and serve all mankind on earth. We answer prayers, help people in the war-torn areas on earth, and help people in sickness and in health, if they are to be blessed. We also impress upon all souls the right things to do by going down to earth and helping people from all walks of life. After we have heard someone's prayers, we help that particular person with the situation in his or her life. We also console people who are grieving after having lost a loved one. In addition to these things, we teach and train the new Cosmic Being to help mankind as well. In addition, we have a karmic board, which helps souls by reviewing what they have completed on earth and highlights what they need to learn or relearn when they return to the Octaves. We have the job of telling them they have not passed the test we gave them in their last lifetime. We are gentle to a point. When a soul is rebellious, then our voices become louder. We get our point across very loudly, since we want all souls, as God has appointed us to facilitate, to make the ascension and believe in God and his oneness.

When a soul comes to earth, its sole reason is to make the ascension and become a believer in God. The soul must live his or her entire life loving God and doing what God wills. If a soul comes to earth and we have given that soul a mission to become a lawyer in order to help a certain amount of people whom we put in his or her pathway, and if that soul refuses to become a lawyer, then when he or she comes up to the karmic board, we tell that soul that he or she failed and didn't help those whom he or she was supposed to help.

The soul could, however, have done a very good job in that life to help others, and believed in God. But the fact remains that when we program by entering data into that soul's computer profile, indicating that he or she should work as a lawyer, for example, and he or she refuses, then we have to tell that individual at the karmic board that he or she has not passed the test of working his or her entire life for God. We do give the soul credit for working during that lifetime, maybe as a cook or a day laborer. That person may have been very kind to his or her neighbors and family, but he or she still did not do what God had intended. The life lesson is to do what God wants a soul to do. In all professions, there are lessons along the way, ones that will teach a soul how to become a better person and help those who come into his or her pathway. The individuals who came into that person's life were supposed to help him or her pass the test.

God set up earth as a kind of college where all souls are to learn, grow, help others, and become kinder and more loving toward each other as they work different professions and travel the road of reincarnation. Many on earth don't believe in reincarnation, but a soul can't learn all the initiations, lessons, and wisdom that he or she must learn to make the ascension if he or she doesn't reincarnate into other lives. Each lifetime is intended to teach the soul various things along the way. How does one act when one is rich? How does one act when one is poor? And how does one act when his or her friend or neighbor has cancer and needs a helping hand? Is that soul going to serve that person and give them a blessing even when he or she can or can't afford it? Will that soul reach out to that other person and help him or her in whatever, capacity they can?

You see, all these tests and or lessons like these are put before mankind. We find that mankind misses so many opportunities to help fellow souls upon this earth. There are those who do help, but they have been helping for many lifetimes. It's the ones who can afford to help but doesn't - that concern us. The lesson was there for those souls to take the opportunity to help another person, perhaps a neighbor or family member, but they failed. This is what we at the karmic board talk to souls about. We recognize those souls that have done much in their lives. They are to return to earth because they have made the ascension and are superheroes in the world. The souls that are blessing others and go unnoticed in life they are the ones that are the Cosmic Beings living on earth whom mankind (the humans) have not recognized, for some odd reason. They do not feel that they are special, but to God they are very special people, as they bless mankind while they have a life on earth.

Many times the karmic board will give a task to those souls that are Cosmic Beings that need to learn additional wisdom for their own enhancement of growth. **Humans look upon an individual as what their eyes see and not what their spiritual body has attained for growth.** A soul for instances that is poor or a street dweller, mankind judges that soul as not being worthy of the standards they were taught in a home environment or within society basic standards, we all conform too emotionally and mentally. Many times Cosmic Beings do not take on a rich life and society thinks they are not a wise soul or they lack the wisdom from God. On the contrary that soul may be learning one small lesson to enrich their growth as a Cosmic Being and coupled with their life they are continuing to work for God and help souls upon this earth.

However, not all Cosmic Beings are rich and famous. Some are, but most are not. The ones who are not are the worker bees in the trenches. We of the karmic board send them down to earth. They work for low wages and have a hard time paying their monthly bills, yet they work for God and bless mankind at their work environment or in their neighborhoods. They work for God, helping to send the message forth for others to follow what they are doing: to helping mankind on earth.

Poverty would not exist on earth if more souls helped and if the government changed a few processes to help the poor—help them find jobs, train them, and provide them with the skills they need to work for a living. Many Cosmic Beings are poor so that God can have them reach the souls in the trenches who are not following God. Indeed, these souls in the trenches some don't believe in God. Sometimes, we send several souls into poor neighborhoods to reveal God to people there. These individuals sacrifice their lives by being Cosmic Beings who don't have to come back to earth to help reveal God to the person who doesn't believe in God and doesn't want to believe in God. So, this is the type of Cosmic Being whom hardly anyone notices on the streets, since the rich Cosmic Being is helping too. But rich Cosmic Beings help in a different capacity, as they don't have the opportunity to reach out to the poor on a daily basis. Only when food is needed does the rich Cosmic Being run to serve the poor.

When someone is rude to a Cosmic Being, who may be a waitress, he or she is making karma. It behooves all of mankind to be nice to everyone, since one never knows to whom one is talking to. Just because a person is rich and beautiful does not mean that he or she is a Cosmic Being. Maybe that individual needed to learn a few things in that life about being rich and famous and also needed to meet a certain person or give the world a message to help all of mankind. Each life is different. What mankind doesn't know is if they started to treat all souls on earth with politeness and respect, as if they were kings or queens, then they would not accumulate extra bad karma. All souls except for Cosmic Beings come to earth to work off their karma and make the ascension. When you see on the news that a certain famous person must appear in court, was hurt in a car accident, or said something rude to target a certain race of people on earth, it is evidence of that famous person's making karma. Maybe that person didn't come to the world with karma, but after exhibiting that behavior, he or she made karma! If you keep your behavior in line with Godly aspects and, respect people and speak cordially to them and you, do your job, and are nice and kind, then you will not make karma. Only the karma that you came into this lifetime with is what you will work off.

Karma can be good or bad. It can be tough, for instance, for the soul whom, if we asked for instance (a soul) to work in the North Pole because he had certain skills as a Cosmic Being or an Angel. That is a hard assignment compared to the assignment in Hawaii. Sometimes, we send souls to school in the Octaves to learn a certain profession so that they can use it to help others. One such profession is becoming a doctor. We may send a doctor to Africa in harsh conditions to treat diseases. Compare this to the doctor working in Beverly Hills, California, where it is very comfortable, where many are rich, and where doctors' fees are high. Generally speaking, a doctor in Africa is not paid as well as a doctor in Beverly Hills, California. A doctor in Africa may not have a lavish house, as some doctors in Beverly Hills do.

Each soul that comes into a body whether a Cosmic Being or a human who has not made the ascension, has trials and lessons to learn, which help souls gain wisdom. Some Cosmic Beings want to help mankind and talk to humans just as I am talking to the instrument while she types what I am saying. To do this, we Angels need to know many things on earth. So we keep in touch with souls on earth and learn more from being involved in our instruments' daily life. I am with my instrument 24/7, so I learn about her bills and, how to pay bills, how to count money, and what her boss task her to do, and what she does at work, what she likes to eat, where she buys her clothes, and how much things cost on earth. And all of that is a lesson for me too, so I can grow in the angelic kingdom and then teach others. One day, as we learn about earth, we Angels can come to earth and embody a human body, and experience life on earth, which, of course, makes us wiser in the angelic kingdom. There are many ways in which we can all grow. This way is one of them, since I, for instance, having never been in a human body. I had to ask my instrument many questions about things upon the earth. It was a great lesson for me. When my instrument needed help to finance her new house and sell her condo, I was there to give her a blessing so that she could move on. We Angels wanted her to move to the country and be in a calm environment so she could write books. That is her karma—to write books. She said, "I can't write a word."

We all laughed and said, "Yes, you can write." And so we began to train and teach her to listen to us so she could write down what we said to her. Now she is very good at automatic writing and well skilled in this task. Still, I remember that she laughed at us when we told her that she was going to write books, asking, "Are you on drugs?"

As an Angel, I asked, "What are drugs?" We both laughed. She explained what drugs were. I said, "No, I have never taken drugs."

Everyone on earth, in the Octaves, and in the angelic kingdom depends on each other somewhat. We all learn and grow from each other when we have experiences, whether they are on earth, in the Octaves, or in the angelic kingdom. In the Octaves and in the higher heavenly world, or the angelic kingdom, more wisdom means more light. When one has more light, one is above others. That is how our ranking system works. All universes share this same ranking system. The more light a soul has the closer to the top he or she is. That soul is also listened to more and may become the leader of the Octaves, the angelic kingdom, the universe, or many universes, depending on how much light and wisdom he or she has. A soul of this type is very highly ranked and teaches others, gives speeches, and helps souls who have less light by providing wisdom and pointing out the lessons they need to learn.

Say that a soul wants to learn to answer prayer. When the soul crosses over from the earth, we teach them to answer all prayers, given that mankind can be very vocal when it comes to prayers. When a prayer comes up from earth, it comes in the form of a ball that has the supplicant's name on it. We look up that person in the computer and find his or her personal profile. We assess his or her karma and then we begin to answer the prayer. For instance, let's say that a woman wants to marry a certain man with whom she is in love with. She tells God that she wants to marry this man. We find in her profile that she is supposed to marry another man, as he will teach her many lessons that will be good for her karma. We don't grant that woman her prayer, but we do make sure that the other man whom she is scheduled to marry comes along in her life and that she falls in love. You see, at the karmic board, we know what events should take place in a person's life. When two souls are about to enter a life on earth, we have the two individuals meet at the karmic board. They sign a contract saying that they, as a team, will do certain things in that life, according to God's will. They know of each other before they meet in life on earth. When they meet on earth, they seem to feel that they know each other—and, to some degree, they do. So, the woman who is praying to marry the wrong man is not granted her prayer. We refuse to answer her prayer about the other person because God has granted her another person to marry instead. This situation is often found on earth. Many are married to the wrong people because they didn't wait long enough to see whom God was going to bring to them. Instead, they rushed in and married the wrong person. At that point, we in the Octaves and the angelic kingdom have to go into the computer system and change both of those individuals' profiles. In a case like this one, the person who married the wrong person is not programmed for the karma that the other person in the relationship might have. The couple begins to fight and argue because they are not programmed to have the karmic experiences that they are supposed to have in the relationship. The marriage eventually ends up being a very unhappy one. Sometimes, these fools stay together when they should divorce. If they left each other, then their lives would straighten out and they would find happiness, even if they had karma with another person. If it were the right karma, the type for which they were scheduled for, then they would have helped their relationship partner.

When two people are not scheduled to be together, there are a lot of signs along the way indicating that these two individuals should separate and move forward with their lives with other partners. Unfortunately, mankind can't see these things. They marry and then blame their failed relationships on God. But these humans were not following their inner gut feelings with which God supplied them to prevent them from jumping into a mistake and marrying the wrong person. However, the humans sometimes don't listen to the soft voice within. Instead, they jump in and get married, and it's a disaster. This is because the couple doesn't share the same experiences and they don't share the karma, which one or both individuals have to overcome and learn from in order to make the ascension.

Let's say that two individuals get married. According to their profiles, one of them is supposed to go through a court experience on earth. This person does something unethical, gets caught, and hires a lawyer. He or she must go through a court hearing, pay the attorney, and fess up to the unethical behavior that caused him or her to be in court in the first place. If the other partner in that relationship was not scheduled to go through a court experience, then it can be extremely difficult for the pair, even on good days. The other soul in the relationship is angry and asks his or her spouse, "How could you be so stupid? Why did you do this?" This soul's response to his or her spouse's behavior is out of character because he or she doesn't understand the karma that his or her partner must face in the court hearing. The other partner didn't sign up for that experience at the karmic board, so it's a foreign concept to that soul. Of course, this causes more irritation and heartache for the soul.

But when two souls are scheduled for the same experience in life, they hang onto each other and become stronger. People who are in unscheduled relationships grow farther apart. After the court verdict is read, the soul who didn't sign up for that karmic experience usually leaves the relationship because he or she was not scheduled for and didn't need that experience in life. The person becomes angry at God. But, really, the person should be angry at him-or herself for marrying the wrong person instead of waiting for the right person to appear. Asking your Light Body to guide all relationships helps the soul avoid pitfalls in unscheduled relationships.

In the next chapter, I will explain, as I mentioned before, since 2010 or the past five years what we in the universe have been going through. I will describe to mankind what happened behind the scenes while everyone on earth was doing what they were supposed to do while living their lives. Maybe, I will answer some of your questions by clarifying things that have happened to us in the Octaves and the angelic kingdom. I will also explain the war of good and evil, which has taken place on earth for the last five years while everyone on the planet was shopping, praying to God, not praying to God, and witnessing floods, earthquakes, mudslides, fires, and tornados, asking, "Where is God in all of this?"

Chapter Two

Earth is a planet of babies. What this means is that mankind as a whole is spiritually undeveloped. In the universes, we have laws. For example, no souls are allowed to attack souls in another universe unless the souls are equally spiritually developed. Most of the time, one universe does not attack another universe. The universes are very, very far apart in miles, but, still, attacks have been known to happen.

Earth is a beautiful planet. It shines with sunlight and is a great size for its inhabitants. It is located close to the Second World called Space. It takes only six or seven weeks to travel to the other universes in the Second World called Space. Each World called Space is separated by a million miles. Planet earth is located in the First World called Space. There are thirteen planets within each First or Second World called Space. Earth is at the edge of the million miles that separates the two worlds. So, now I have provided you with a few logistics about the universes that mankind has never tapped into. People have a reason to continue searching for other universes and seek the information they desire. What they desire to explore and study other planets, which, by the way, are not as pretty as earth is today.

At this point, I will give the reader a history lesson about what has been happening in these universes, since mankind is unaware of many things. People are so busy with life—shopping, attending church, praying to God, raising children, and supporting their children's efforts in sports or school activities, all of which are great behaviors. We Angels realize that people's lives are busy with daily activities. For example, when I follow my instrument around, I see that she is busy each day with her work environment and supporting her bosses. Then she has her work at home, which includes writing books, doing yard work, picking up the dry-cleaning, doing the grocery shopping, cleaning the house, and washing the car. She rarely has time for other things in her life. After she does all of the things mentioned above, it's time to start all over again. She has a daily one-hour commute to and from work. While she is driving to work, I and the other Angels talk to her about life in the angelic kingdom or in the Octaves. Five years ago, when she could finally hear us and type what we were saying, we started having her take down our messages and typing them up at the end of the day. Some of those messages were sixteen pages long. This built her skill level. We would explain to her what was happening in the universes, with other souls, and with other planets. We explained that many of the good souls were seeking help and a place of safety, since the evil ones were attacking and taking over many planets in many universes. The evil ones are those souls that once believed in God and now don't want to follow God's orders. They built their armies many millions of years ago. We all know that they are out there, but people on earth have never dealt with them, since we have universal laws to spiritually protect the innocent, young, underdeveloped souls that exist on earth.

There is so much more than one needs to believe. When souls cross over, they all complain, e.g., "Why didn't my minister know this information?" And, "Why don't I remember this information when I enter a human body?" Some souls do remember, but most don't. This is because we Angels want human beings to pass the test without knowing the answers ahead of time. The soul's disconnect is very strong, and causes people to block out the memory of past lives, including who they are in the Octaves or angelic kingdom. Some souls on earth are actually Angels, Cosmic Beings, or BEINGS. The last is a different type of soul that is very intelligent. It comes from another universe. Only the Cosmic Being is from earth, or the human kingdom. God made those particular souls for the human kingdom. They reside on earth to learn and grow spiritually.

As I said before, we have universal laws. No one is allowed to attack the babies, which are on earth, because they are not spiritually developed, it would be as if an adult attacked a two year old child for not balancing the check book. The understanding is not developed. And mankind as a whole doesn't believe in being spiritual. Only if a minister explains to the congregation the wisdom of God to them do they, perhaps, believe? But on the whole, they do not believe in God. They hear the words in church and once they leave the Sunday session their behavior is sometimes less than Godly. So if one truly believes their behavior would be an example of Godliness daily.

People are given certain gifts. One of this instrument's gifts is that she can type what we are saying to her. She is writing this book for mankind, to show people that writing is one of the many gifts mankind can have. Another gift is heightened awareness. When a person walks into a room, those who have the gift of heightened awareness can feel that individual's vibration. Still, most of mankind cannot do this. But this instrument can tell when a person is lying to her or if a person's vibration is horrible. These gifts, two of which I have named, can be developed on earth. This, of course, can enhance a person's awareness, and then that person can use the gifts to his or her advantage.

In 2010 while we were training the instrument to type for us, we were attacked and had to call for help from BEINGS in the other universes, asking them to come to earth and teach us to fight the evil ones, who had converged on us and began attacking us. We lost many at that time because the Cosmic Beings would not even dream of not believing in God or have learned how to fight with other souls. The Cosmic Beings were at a disadvantage due to their innocence of evil. They built a hideout by digging a hole in the center of the earth. They ran to the hole (as they called it) to protected themselves, when the evil ones came to attack the souls in the angelic kingdom and the Octaves. Many BEINGS came to teach us and show us that a soul could receive many gifts if it became spiritually developed. The most advanced spiritually developed souls who have many gifts are called BEINGS. God made this type of soul second. The first type of soul he made was the Angel. When they landed, took over, and started to run the Octaves and help the Cosmic Beings, we found that many souls in the Octaves had joined the evil ones. We annihilated the Cosmic Beings (who were evil) about ten thousand of them went to the ovens. We were all crying and hysterical since none of us knew about this army called the evil ones. As time progressed, the BEINGS began to teach all of the Cosmic Beings and Angels how to fight and protect themselves. The hole in the center of earth was never used again.

The BEINGS also taught us how to manage a war and use strategy. We asked all the soldiers who had crossed over to help us strategize to win the war between good and evil that was upon us, while earth's inhabitants were shopping, entirely unaware of what was going on above their heads. This war, consisting of nonstop fighting, took place daily. It took us two days to fight the evil ones since they came at us with such vengeance and hatred. And, it took us many hours, sometimes weeks, of nonstop fighting to save our own lives and mankind's lives. If we had let the evil ones win, then they would have come to earth and started killing mankind. We couldn't let that happen. One of our jobs in the heavenly world is to protect, guide, and help mankind, and we were bound and determined not to let the evil ones succeed in their endeavor.

As the battles continued, we began to ask questions about the evil ones—since *none* of us in the heavenly world, which exists above earth, knew about the evil ones, and we received a history lesson about them. This is what was told to us.

Millions of years ago, God set up all the universes so souls could grow beyond their wildest dreams and become godly creatures or souls. The word *God* is a title, just like "president of the United States" or "president of [such-and-such] corporation" it's a title. These souls are not above the law. Each soul in every universe can grow to become a god. One group of souls refused to follow God's universal laws as God wanted all universes organized under a Godly aspect. These souls and God had strong words about how the universes should be run. The conversation between God and the other souls ended abruptly with words of war against God. Thousands of years ago, there was a great divide in the universes. We had the godly souls and we had the souls that were against God. They wanted to take over and rule all universes in an evil fashion. And for thousands of years we have been fighting the evil one's ever since. These evil souls now live on many planets all across the twenty-six universes, thirteen in the First World Called Space and thirteen in the Second World Called Space.

In 2010 we had our first taste of evil coming to earth and setting up camp. None of us in the heavenly kingdom were aware of them. They began to manipulate the weather and terrorize the Cosmic Beings, creating battle after battle. Pretending to be nice, godly souls, they came to the Octaves under the guise of helping us, saying that they believed in God. They were eventually exposed as being evil, although they caused havoc within the Octaves and killed other godly souls. It was horrible. We were fighting our guts out and trying to make sense of what was happening. We were ignorant of the fact that the evil ones were able to play games with us. To our dismay, we found that they were masterminds at being evil. As I said before, we annihilated them in the ovens. This all happened under our noses until we became sharper in our tactics and began trusting each other to find out who was evil and who was not. This went on for a few years. As it continued, we became much more skilled in our use of tactics. We also became more aware and began to spot these evil souls. In addition, we began to defend ourselves much better. This led us to learn and grow. And grow we did, to the point where we now have a lot of light from the wisdom gained by being in that horrible situation.

During this war, the Angels and Cosmic Beings were introduced to the BEINGS for the first time in the history of the universes. The BEINGS were all living on other planets and influenced the second type of soul that God had created for the universes. The BEINGS stand very tall and are very bright souls. Having had previous experience with evil, they began to teach us how to handle the horrible evil souls that lied to us, played games with us, and tricked us. Of course, we annihilated those evil souls. Once we finally rid ourselves of the evil within the Octaves, we felt sad, since the evil ones had pretended to be our friends. Some were our family members. We sent them all to the ovens because they wanted to kill us if we didn't submit to their threats and join them. We said, *"Never!"* As the playing field became more balanced and we as Cosmic Beings and Angels felt more confident in ourselves, in our fighting abilities, and in our chances of winning all of the battles, it seemed that the world was not improving.

We were still seeing mass destruction on earth, what with the catastrophic weather and the wars breaking out. We knew that the evil ones were casting veils over the earth so that mankind would react to those veils and become confused. The evil ones created more destruction on earth by waging wars and controlling the weather—creating tornados, earthquakes, and mudslides to hurt mankind.

During this time we were introduced to the Queen of Queens who came to the earth 2,000 years ago, to help us fight the evil ones that were parked above the Octaves without us every realizing they were there. So all our efforts at times were foiled, due to them being above us, and watching every move or thought or plan we had. The Queens family, her father the Seed of God and her seven brothers and sisters were there to help her annihilate the evil ones as we carried on our daily lives not realizing, as I said before that the evil leadership was living above the Octaves. The Queen is a million years old and has been traveling around many universes annihilating the evil upon many planets. When she came to the earth the evil ones followed her (as she was hiding out) to try and annihilate her. They knew she was extremely powerful and had grown as she traveled around on her own, helping all other planets' inhabitants to defeat the evil that was living among them. As the Queen grew in wisdom and light, remember that wisdom creates light, and that a soul can't hide its light. Unless that soul concentrates to master the gift of hiding one's light otherwise, as a soul walks around their light will shine. Those that are not as high or carry the same light as another high soul, that individual soul, could be burned if they walk to close to the soul that has the huge aura of light. The Queen when she shines her light can light up the sky.

Eventually, she revealed herself to us in the Octaves and began to help us to strategize and annihilate the evil ones when they came to attack us. The Queen told us the story of her life, saying that she escaped from the evil ones since they were hunting for her because she refused to join them in the war against God. She came to earth to hide and help the innocent souls who have no idea that evil exist or battles existed in the heavenly world as well. While souls on earth don't have to believe in God, the Queen felt that it was her job to protect the innocent souls who were living in the heavenly world or on earth since they were babies. Actually, those of us in the heavenly world are or were babies too. The Queen began to teach us how to acquire more wisdom and outsmart the evil ones. Since that time, we have annihilated trillions upon trillions of evil souls. We recently annihilated the evil leadership team for whom the Queen knew they had been hunting for her the last two thousand years, ever since she came to earth and lived undercover.

A soul can suppress their light at times. The Queen did a very good job with this, as she is advanced, given her gifts and wisdom. Her father and family were also advanced in light, gifts and wisdom. If you have these gifts within, then all children born to you also have those gifts. Each child or soul knows this and begins to develop the gifts. Since the gifts manifests within a particular individual, those who have them grow up to develop or practice those gifts and bring them to the surface, as we call it. This way, souls use their gifts and gain more wisdom as they develop and grow into adults. It takes thousands of years to develop as a powerful soul. Every day, a soul works on increasing its wisdom by helping mankind and the heavenly world. These souls take classes and listen to other wise souls that are living on a specific planet or within a particular universe. All souls in possession of much light are regarded as rare and are subsequently well protected, since it is God's will that they be. The Queen is one of those who are protected. No one can stand in her light. When she walks around the Octaves, she hides her light so we can walk past her. If we stood in her magnificent light, we would burn up and die. The Queen is so powerful that if anyone rushes up to her, she can hold her hand up and kill that individual. While her light is powerful, she is very kind and brilliant. All of us love to listen to her when she delivers speeches about various topics including the evil ones and when they will come to attack us. She can wipe out trillions of evil ones with one swing of the hand; her light is that magnificent. Whereas, most souls can only take out one or two souls depending on their power and growth of light, as well as millions of souls at a time. The queen can annihilate trillions at one time.

For the last million years or so, the Queen has helped many souls in all universes by battling the evil leadership. It is rare for a soul to leave and venture out on her own, being so young and a female too, it's very dangerous. The Queen is very beautiful. Everyone stares at her when they see her because she is so gorgeous. She has long, curly blonde hair and big blue eyes. Most of the time, she wears diamond dresses, except when she is battling with the evil ones. In all the universes, there is another law for one who has that much power and light. Rare ones like the Queen are allowed to wear diamond dresses, which set them apart from other souls and show them as being very high. No one is allowed to wear a diamond dress unless he or she carries a certain amount of light. Light is measured by the size of their aura in inches, feet or miles. Everyone knows who these souls are. All woman souls want a diamond dress, and so we work very hard to gain as much light and wisdom as we can. We can rule a planet or a universe when we gain enough wisdom and light. Just as you on earth have a ranking system, in all universes we have a ranking system—and all souls on every planet know these rules and laws of each universe. Just as a human on earth knows to stop the car at red lights and keep the car within the white lines while driving, souls in other realms know what rules they have to follow to remain safe. The information I mentioned above is common knowledge to all of us in all universes, but it's not known on earth.

When the Queen was finally revealed, she told us the story about her family leading the way against the evil battles and wars all across the universes. She mentioned that she needed to go undercover. Being undercover helped us without our knowing that she was in the Octaves for the past two thousand years. She is a very strong Angel who rules this heavenly world. All bow to her five foot frame. Her title is Queen of Queens. We have many other queens, but they don't carry the light or wisdom that she does. She is above all the kings and queens of all universes. Her subjects love and adore her. She helped many universes while she was on the run. She has made many friends. When the Octaves needed help and guidance to fight the evil that was coming our way, she called upon her friends in other universes, who came running to planet earth, where they have stayed for the last five years, teaching the Cosmic beings many things. Those who did come to rescue us and teach us to fight lost their planets, and also their family and friends, to the evil ones. When the evil ones come to a planet, they begin with a surprise attack. After they killed many souls on that planet, they locked up the Godly souls whom they did not kill into work camps. When the godly souls who were locked up had the chance to escape the work camps, they fled to another planet and then, eventually, came to the Octaves in order to help mankind. All the souls that are above planet earth are very aware of what the evil ones can do to a civilization in a matter of hours. These souls brought their wisdom to the Octaves and Angelic kingdom, along with the history of their battles. They taught us what the evil ones were capable of doing, and we learned very quickly how to save ourselves and mankind.

The Octaves and the angelic kingdom now have over a hundred million souls helping mankind and fighting the evil ones daily. Recently, we had a victory. We annihilated additional leadership group of evil. At one time there were trillions of evil ones above us. The Queen helped us to strategize our moves and win our battles. She saw where we could overtake them, and we did as she suggested. Now, finally, after all those years of fighting daily battles, we realize that our light has expanded, and we are over throwing the evil as we venture out into the First World Called Space and annihilating there planets. The Queen told us they were leaving the Second World Called Space, moving to the First World Called Space, and joining the other evil camps. We are thrilled that we annihilated the upper-level evil leadership team, and as BEINGS, Cosmic Beings and Angels continue to fight and battle to save themselves and mankind we are winning with Gods support and love. **God is always on his thrown.** He has thanked us many times for our valiant efforts to rid our planet earth from the evil leadership that once lived above the octaves.

I wanted to tell the reader the real story about the last millions of years and say that evil is alive. The evil ones have not given up on taking over earth. We will never give up on believing in God or protecting mankind from the evil forces that are out there. They are always plotting and planning their next move to annihilate a planet or a civilization. They can't withstand being in the Queen's presence, as her light is so bright. At times, she will lie down at the top of the heavenly world and shine her light, which spreads for more than six hundred thousand miles. Everyone in the heavenly world can stand underneath it and be healed. If you are evil then you will be burned up—so, she shines her light for the evil ones to touch and be burned up. This is another method used to fight the daily battles. When she does this, those in the hospital for surgery or an illness are instantly healed. She does go down to earth at times in war-torn areas and heals those people when the evil ones are not attacking us. She gives us lessons on how to help mankind, as she is a very kind queen. When you see a bright light in the sky and don't know what it is, it's the Queen of Queens shining her light on the areas of the world that need healing.

At this time, all of us in the Octaves, Cosmic Beings, and BEINGS feel that we are beyond the worst of it. Some battles continue, but since we have annihilated the evil leaders, it will take many years for them to become strong and fight us again. However, we will continue to monitor the situation. As the evil ones continue to come our way, as they are all moving out from the Second World Called Space to join the First World Called Space evil ones, and flying around earth, then we will continue to annihilate them to, protect earth's inhabitants, and still believe in God. Those of you, who are reading this book, please continue to pray for us, for your prayers do help and protect us. We continue to pray for, help, and save mankind to experience the happiness, hope, and joy that we want all of you to have. You would not be able to have those things if the evil ones were allowed to take over your planet. We in the angelic kingdom and the Octaves also fight for our happiness and joy—and for our love of God too. Our lives are somewhat bereft of hope, happiness, and joy at this time because we are constantly battling the evil ones. In our realms, no babies are being born and none of us are getting married because we are too busy battling with the evil ones on mankind's behalf.

Chapter Three

Now I have told you about the troubles and battles with the evil ones that we are experiencing in the Octaves and the angelic kingdom. It has posed a situation in the Octaves. In the last five years, who have crossed over? They attended church on earth, and the ministers to whom they listened to told the congregations that the heavenly world is calm and peaceful and that, there, all souls will shake hands with the Christ once they cross over. The ministers said that all souls would be floating around, that the streets would be paved with gold, that souls would have angel wings, and that souls would see their family members who crossed over before. All the stories that the new crossovers told us raised an issue. We had to tell them that some of the information they heard is not true. There are no paved-with-gold streets in the Octaves or the angelic kingdom. Yes, souls can see Jesus when he is out battling with the rest of us, but he will not shake anyone's hand unless he or she (is a soul) who has made the ascension in that lifetime; otherwise, that individual will be a worker bee, as many are in the Octaves, and will join the ranks. If the soul has light, then it is higher than the average person. If it doesn't have light or wisdom, then it is found among the ranks of the worker bees, learning wisdom. None of these souls has leadership power and so they can't lead anyone in the Octaves or the angelic kingdom. All souls must have light to lead and become directors or managers. Being famous on earth doesn't give a soul any extra privileges. Just like everyone else, famous people must fall into line, depending on where their souls fit on the light scale or in the ranking system that we have set up in all universes. Those who are lighted have the power to be leaders in some capacity, but new crossover souls are not leaders. This is where the ranking system comes into play. Mankind is not developed spiritually. When one crosses over as a soul, he or she works as others work and also takes orders, given that he or she does not have the light required to be a leader. Most souls that cross over realize that most of the things they were told in church are not true.

I am writing this book for this reason to clarify the differences of what a minister says at the pulpit and we in the Octaves and Angelic kingdom actually how we live, and all the stories of souls that we deal with daily to tell the average soul who lives on earth, **"Call upon your own Light Body and begin to have your Light Body guide you and help you with daily tasks or other things you need to do.** Ask your Light Body to help you with your development so you can learn spiritual concepts and change your thinking. In other words, think about any of your behavior that might need changing." We have funny stories about many souls that, once they crossed over, were entirely unaware of what they did wrong on earth. When they come to the karmic board, we go over those things with them and show them where they were wrong. We mention that they never gained much light while living on earth because they rarely treated fellow souls with kindness. They were sometimes rude or nasty to other people or wanted to avenge an injustice. They thought that they were entitled to attack someone else, secretly or openly, but they read the circumstances incorrectly. If they had called on a Light Body, then the Light Body would have pulled them from their bodies at night and explained the situation. That information would have stayed in their auras. They would have understood things at a cellular level and would not have attacked the person who was giving them the karma that they had come to earth to receive. It behooves all souls on earth to call upon their Light Bodies. The Light Body will start to guide them and direct them toward the right pathway, as these souls need to move if they are not on the right pathway.

Being on the right pathway includes making changes in one's life. When a soul marries then changes come to each of the souls involved in the new relationship. The center of all marriages should be God, praying daily for god to guide each other in their future plans together. These things could be buying a house, having children, changing jobs, and being financially savvy. **Creating debt is against God's law.** There were times in my instrument's life when she decided to charge things on a credit card. For example, her tires needed to be replaced or the car needed repairs. When she charges an item on her credit card, she quickly begins to pay off the debt. She stops going out and spending money in order to save for the credit card balance that she needs to pay so as not to have that debt. It may take her months to pay a particular charge, so she rarely goes anywhere. For you reading this book, pay off all of your debts, including your mortgage (if possible) and other monthly bills, such as your electricity, gas, and day-care bills. Those are the only bills that any soul on earth needs to have.

My instrument pays those monthly bills. She uses any money left over, which isn't much, to buy her groceries. We want all of mankind on earth to realize that as long as they have debts because they were greedy for things they couldn't afford, they are struck with the worry of paying off the bills. This type of worry doesn't leave time for a human being on earth to think about God. People constantly worry about their debt, but God wants all humans to think on him, not on the debt that they incurred because they desired or were greedy for something else when they had plenty at home. God wants all humans to be free from debt, apart from bills for living expenses, so they can be generous with their money and help those in need. This way, when they see someone in need, they can help that person. God desires all humans on earth to change their behavior and live without bills so that they can show their kindness and generosity to others. If everyone on the face of the earth would start paying off their credit-card debt and learn to live within their budgets, then credit card companies would have to find a new way of doing business. As we look at CEOs and presidents, we see that they are not "doing" without much—they are living off of other people's stupid decisions and undisciplined behavior. Lenders can charge high interest rates, take the profit, and use it to live lavish lives. However, not all CEOs are guilty of this, but many are. And while I am on the topic of finances, I will say that some higher-ups take bonuses for themselves and lay off their workers. They receive astronomical bonuses from the company coffers. Only the elite receive these bonuses. But these CEOs or executive vice presidents are making karma by not sharing any bonuses with the entire company staff. If the company would share and give bonuses to every employee, then it would become fair. That is what God wants: fairness. Mankind has a ranking system, or a caste system, within its corporations. Those at the top are fortunate to receive bonuses, while those who are not at the top are subject to layoffs. The executive staff still collects huge bonuses, some of them in the millions of dollars, with no regard for trying to keep the staff and, instead, laying them off. We realize that life is hard on earth and that it's difficult to stop shopping and, instead, stay at home or ride a bike. It is tough to stop doing things that cost money and buying things to try and make yourself happy, but all humans on earth need to start paying off their bills.

 My instrument was living in a very small condo. She decided to move to the countryside. So, she began to list all her bills that were not living expenses and stopped going out with her friends. She began to pay off her bills. Paying bills one by one, she succeeded. It was boring for her, but she hung in there, bound and determined to rid her life of debt. On her desk was a list that she looked at weekly. She checked off each debt one by one as the balance became zero. It took her over seven years to pay off her debt since, as she would say, life "hit" her with other things, such as medical bills that her insurance would not pay and the car-repair expenses. She was set back at times, but she continued to pay her bills for seven years. When she was out driving one day, I impressed upon her that she should drive to the countryside. There were new homes being built there, so she stopped in and talked to one of the realtors. The realtor told her what she needed to offer for a down payment and how much her monthly payment would be. She saw that buying a home was achievable. She called her realtor in her old neighborhood, and he came over and assessed her condo. She had three weeks to repaint and move into storage the huge furniture that she has had for over twenty years. She put the condo on the market, and it sold in one day. For a month, she rented the condo from the new owners. After that, she moved into her new townhouse in the countryside, which is where we wanted her because it's calm and quiet—a place for her to write with me for the next few years while she is on earth. When we told her that she was going to write books out in the country, she laughed at us, but here she is, writing this book. She enjoys it very much and says, "It stops me from shopping."

Take up a hobby that interests you, but make sure that it isn't an expensive one. Pursue your hobby instead of wandering through stores or malls all day long, using shopping as a form of entertainment. You will be surprised to learn how long it takes to pay off a bill by remitting only the minimum payment each month. You will also be surprised when you discover the percentage rates that companies charge you to carry a balance on a credit card. When you see what you are really paying, you will be motivated to pay off those credit cards as fast as you can.

As the instrument was taking more of an interest in her credit-card debt and started to look at the interest rates she was charged, she was floored and began to pay down those balances as fast as she could. During that time, she didn't go to a shopping mall except to buy a gift for someone else. In the Octaves, we have a huge store and workers who make all our clothes. We have much to choose from. When any soul, as a new crossover, comes to our realm, he or she needs clothes and undergarments and so goes to the store to pick out things to wear. The clothes are free. New crossovers always say, "This is so much fun!" They love to shop but soon realize that they don't have much time to do it after that first initial trip because they become so busy helping mankind, learning where everything is located in the Octaves, setting up a house (or the house they share with others), and working to learn how to answer prayer. There surprised to find that we have computer profiles for all souls on earth, including the history of all their past lives, what they have learned, and what they continually need to learn as they perform their job, or tour of duty, on earth. Cosmic Beings are given a tour of duty because they have made the ascension, but a soul that has not made the ascension takes another life, wherein it must try to pass the life test that it failed in the last life. That is the difference. All alcoholics, for instance, come back to another life in order to stop drinking and detach from alcohol. They, as all souls do, need to be attached to God and godly beliefs and also be kind and generous with others who don't have the means to buy the things they need. So, when you see a need to buy someone food at the grocery store, do it, as my instrument has done in the past for a single mother struggling with day-care bills and paying high rent. People like that woman could use your help in paying their bills. If you can afford it, then do it for someone. If you see a person on the street who is clearly homeless, then offer him or her a meal and help if you can.

The instrument comes from California. Certain areas in California are home to street dwellers. Many times, other Californians help those street dwellers with food or money, if they can afford it. Now that the instrument lives on the East Coast, we don't see many homeless people on the streets since it's very cold in the winter months, whereas California is sunny and mostly warm all year round.

Once new crossovers awake in the hospital, they are met by a nurse who asks, "What is your name?" We look in the computer to find their real name and see if their real family is in the Octaves or the angelic kingdom. If so, then they need to be moved to the angelic kingdom's hospital. They are so surprised to be met by such nice souls and beings who explain what happened to them and say that they have crossed over, telling them that they are fine. If they have family, then the hospital staff calls the family to come help with the explanation of what happened. They are then reintroduced to their real family, the one from which they originally came (the earth family was the one that they had to learn lessons from. Otherwise, it was convenient for that soul to enter into that family to accomplish the goal it was supposed to achieve while living on earth).

Most families on earth have one or two members who are Cosmic Beings or Angels. They teach others about life and being godly. Also, don't discount the soul in the handicapped body. He or she is usually a Cosmic Being or Angel who is helping that family learn about unconditional love. Maybe the last stage of that soul's or family's growth is learning unconditional love. The handicapped person in that house is teaching the family that lesson.

As a soul begins to grow, it must learn many lessons, including treating fellow humans with respect, love, and kindness. Next, the soul goes through a soul-growth initiation, which is very difficult and becomes progressively harder. All of the lessons are about love. Losing a loved one is an initiation too. While they are on earth, most souls who lost a loved one early in life (sometimes, later in life) are very high. They learn to love God when their heart is breaking. That is very difficult, because most souls get very upset at God when they lose a loved one. But remember, when you go to the karmic board and sign up for a life on earth, part of that life may include losing a loved one. You will see the deceased person on the other side when you eventually cross over.

The soul must stand firm and realize that things are happening in its life for a reason. The reason will be revealed when the soul crosses over, as I said. When a soul enters a human body, its memory is disconnected from who it really is in the Octaves or angelic kingdom. All souls must take the last test of growth, the soul initiation, which is all about love. When the soul is advanced enough to learn these lessons, it knows that it is taking part in an initiation. Souls pass the test by not hating God and not blaming God for the injustices that might have prevailed in his or her life. Many souls on earth at this time are very high and think that they do not inhabit bodies. But that is not true. When they cross over, we tell them that their life was difficult because they passed the initiation test and were presented with very difficult challenges. Most souls, when they reach a state of being very high, can pass these tests without making any mistakes. I sit at times and watch the news with the instrument. She comments when a woman has lost a child or a husband in some tragic event. There are many news stories of souls who have lost loved ones. The instrument starts to cry and says, "Oh my. That person has a long, hard road to travel for an initiation." And that is true. The instrument has had much heartache in passing her soul's initiation. She has done very well, but it's not been without many tears along the way. She realizes, as she watches the news, which others are going through the same things she went through earlier in her life. We surround the person mentioned on the news with many Angels and begin to talk to that person, helping him or her understand that it's an initiation for his or her soul's growth. We say that these initiations are very hard, very tearful, and sometimes very complex. The person does come to develop some calmness about the situation when he or she learns why a loved one had to cross over. These souls do come to God later in life. They pass the test if they still love God. And when their family members cross over, we explain to them why they all passed a hard initiation and what happened. We say that they are growing spiritually and have made it to the next step on the ladder, if I can say it that way and the reader can understand me. All souls, no matter in which universe they are living at are always growing. They are always trying to gain more wisdom and light in order to become high souls so that, one day, they can become leaders and rule over a planet or universe. It takes much wisdom and love to be a leader and guide a group of trillions of souls to greater growth.

 The Queen of Queens, whom I mentioned in the previous chapter, is one such soul. She has ruled three universes for about twenty thousand years. When we were—as we still are— having troubles with the evil ones attacking us daily, those who knew that she was living above earth all rushed to be under her tutelage, since she is well-known for being one of the greatest leaders any universe has ever had.

The story is told that she ruled one universe for twenty thousand years and had all souls so advanced in wisdom that they could rule other planets. She had trained them well. She is known for her famous speeches, to which we have had the privilege of listening, and uses humor and wit to get her points across. About three years ago, the Queen gave a speech about not having sex in the Octaves, as all souls the Octaves are not allowed to cohabitate before they are married. Every soul in every universe abides by this rule. Some of the souls in the Octaves were very rebellious souls, and who were cohabitating or sneaking around to have sex with each other out of wedlock. Since the Queen is very aware, she gave a speech one night and shocked everyone by saying that this was taking place in the Octaves. None of us knew that this was happening right under our noses. The Queen of Queens gave them several days to move into separate dwellings and discontinue having sex when not married. Everyone, about five hundred souls, who was guilty of this behavior was caught and had to change living situations. One soul said that he was not going to change. (We see what is in everyone's aura.

If one is married, then we don't see that he or she had sex with his or her spouse. But if one is not married, then we see when that soul has had sex. We know who is married and who is not.) This one soul was bound and determined to defy the Queen. She called him out in front of the audience and asked, "Whom are you sleeping with?" Now, this was in front of millions of Cosmic Beings in our huge auditorium.

The soul replied, "I am not sleeping with anyone."

We all laughed. The Queen asked, "Do you know why everyone is laughing?"

He said, "No."

The Queen said, "Because those of us who are advanced can see what is in a soul's aura, and your aura shows that you are having sex with someone."

He turned white and asked, "Well, now what?"

Everyone laughed. The Queen said, "You will stop or else be put into the oven. We cannot allow anyone not to follow God's laws in the Octaves."

The male soul said, "Okay, I will stop."

The Queen said, "You will move out of your partner's house too—tonight."

He asked, "How do you know these things?"

The Queen answered, "Because I have many gifts that I use to rule a universe. Since you have as much light as a minnow, you can't see what I see. You don't have the light to see others or the truth. You are still learning how to grow as a soul."

The man had to move out of the woman's house. The woman was embarrassed too since she was doing something that was against the law of God.

This story brings me to a point. On earth, those who are living with each other are breaking God's laws. I know that there are many. Whether they are in love or not, they need to change that behavior. Afterward, they will be blessed. I see that some famous people on earth are living with others to whom they are not married. They are learning things in the settings in which they are placed. At times, when God or the karmic board sends a soul down to earth, we at the karmic board become very creative with that life in order to teach the soul what it needs to do (or not do) for God. When a soul that has cheated someone else and comes to us from earth, we sometimes send that soul back down to earth so it can experience the same type of cheating—either being taken from or manipulated.

This is a way for that soul to repay back the karma they once gave to another in a past life. For instance, let's say that a man encounters a woman whom he finds attractive. The two go to the karmic board and decide what type of life the man should have, one that will show him that lying, taking from another, and manipulating another is wrong. The karmic board gives the woman directions and puts them into her profile so she acts a certain way. The man agrees to learn from this experience that is designed by the karmic board. The two people in question meet on earth and move in together. They are not happy, but they make it work. The man is unhappy but doesn't realize that the woman is manipulating him. Of course, their neighbors see it, but the man does not. The woman bears children, and the man is in shock that the woman didn't discuss it with him that she wanted another child. He finally gets the message that he is miserable, not in love, and being taken in this relationship. Everyone looks at the woman as if she is horrible, but she is doing a job for God, teaching this man about not manipulating people, since he did this to another soul in his last life. The man leaves the relationship. When his head clears, he tells himself that he was had, used, and manipulated—and that is exactly what God wanted him to see in the woman's behavior. Remember, the man did the same thing to another person in a past life. After he leaves his wife, he eventually finds another woman who is the opposite of the first woman. He is blessed with happiness and love, although, of course he has to continue to pay child support to his first partner. But he learned his lesson. And this is one among the many tough lessons of life. *No* person on earth has the ability to fairly judge another since the karmic board is very creative in giving out karma—so souls won't repeat damaging behavior on earth or in the Octaves.

We in the Octaves work as a team. We must be able to trust all souls that live in the Octaves just as we trust all Angels. When a soul exhibits the horrible behavior of lying to, cheating, or manipulating another, the Octaves demand that the soul stop that behavior. Souls like this are not allowed to behave in such a way while they're in the Octaves. They are sent down to earth to work off their karma. If they don't learn from past experiences, then we eventually tell them, "This is your last life, and we must see improvement before we can proceed any further with your growth." We say this because there comes a time in those souls' lives when they don't want to grow, don't want to believe in God, don't want to take the initiations, don't want to be kind, don't want to stop lying, and won't work because they are very lazy. Then, we say, "This is the end of the road." We have huge ovens into which we place these souls. Once we light the fire, they are burned up within a few minutes. To the reader, this may seem harsh, but we can't use a rebellious soul. Everyone must follow God. They start by doing what God wants them to do on earth. We give them many lives—and I mean many lives—plus many chances to change their behavior. Most souls start to realize that they need to change, but there are those who don't want to change. If they don't change, then they go to the ovens. We immediately annihilate anyone who is evil and has been talking to another evil one in the garden area. No one in the angelic kingdom is allowed to talk to an evil soul. Everyone knows that if they are caught talking to the evil ones, they are immediately sent to the ovens—and that is the end. Their family members all cry and become hysterical, but that is the law in the Octaves.

Earth is a school that teaches all souls what they will face once they cross over. They are taught and trained again and again, and then they are sent down to earth to try to master their behavior. They are helped along the way by their personal Light Body and the Angels. When they cross over, they are rewarded with a better life. Some are not rewarded with another life. These souls will stay in the Octaves and go back to school before they are allowed to have another life on earth.

Lately, we have been doing many soul exchanges on earth. We watch those Cosmic Beings who have children on earth, and we help them in their daily lives. If the children are acting out and the Cosmic Being is not doing what he or she is supposed to do on earth, then we do a soul exchange, putting another soul in the body. We bring up the rebellious soul and begin to teach it what it was doing wrong. Recently, one Cosmic Being wanted his son and daughter to come home so he could begin to train and teach them to become better citizens of Earth. Neither of them was very nice, and neither got even one of the lessons that the karmic board set up for them. Both of them are basically bright humans. The son, very bright, never got the hint about what he was doing wrong! So, the Cosmic Being said, "Bring them home, and I will begin to train them and teach them. I feel that we were sending souls down to earth too soon, without a proper foundation of believing in God."

When the male and female awoke, they wondered, *Where am I?* The nurse came over and introduced herself to them. Once they dressed, their father came into the hospital and introduced himself to his adult children. The children looked at him as if he were nuts. When a new crossover awakes, he or she doesn't retain a memory, except for the memory of being on earth. When the two children wanted to know where they were, their father, a Cosmic Being, explained to them that they were brother and sister and were now in the Octaves because their souls had been exchanged. He mentioned that he pulled them from earth and placed other souls in their bodies because the two of them were basically whores on earth and he was disgusted with their behavior.

The daughter spoke up and said, "I was looking for a man."

The son said, "I was not looking for anyone."

The Cosmic Being said, "You are both wrong. You should never use anyone on earth for your own pleasure!" Since that time, which was several months ago, the son and daughter have learned much. They see where they were wrong and how they went about life all wrong. They realize how they hurt and manipulated many people in their travels.

It takes about three weeks for a soul's memory to return after the individual has crossed over from Earth's atmosphere. During that time, the soul gets used to being in the Octaves and eventually learns how to walk. Given that not all souls have feet, one needs to learn how to move about and do so with grace, without being a klutz. I say this with fondness.

As the two new crossovers were talking to their Cosmic Being father, they were reminded of their behavior. We have ways of showing all souls pictures of what they did to others on earth—how they misread the circumstances, hurt a person very badly, and made karma. It's like showing a movie of the person's life, one that is very real. All souls are in shock when we bring out the screen and show them what they did and didn't do on earth and who they hurt in the meantime. We illuminate that they were never sorry for their behavior.

The son was the first one to look at the screen. He saw his actions and observed how nasty he was to a certain woman and his daughter on earth, who is a beautiful, smart, kind child. He mistreated her with his words, telling her how lazy she was when she was not lazy at all. He had a few women friends whom he was sleeping with. He lied to all of them. One particular woman stayed around him for years. He couldn't seem to get rid of her, no matter what he said, which was sometimes cruel and rude. He thought that, all that time, the woman was in love with him, but she loved to toy with him. She knew that there was another woman who liked him too. The first one was very kind and nice; she also had grace and class. The woman who was toying with him made sure that she was often at his door. It became a headache for him. He berated and yelled at her, thinking, *she must love me. That is why she won't leave. Any other woman would have left by now.*

Eventually, she did leave. When he saw himself on the screen yelling at her, telling her off, and not handling the situation well, he also saw that the woman was not in love with him and was thrilled to be through with him after the big fight they had on Valentine's Day. He was horrified. All this time, he thought she was in love with him, but he found out that she only stayed around because of this other, beautiful woman who loved him very much and was kind. He did have a relationship with that other woman eventually.

He wondered, while he was dating the other woman, *"Why didn't I see this before?*" "He said it aloud: "How come I didn't see this before?" "The women who loved me and, the other women toying with me?"

He thought her behavior was showing him that she was in love with him. Unfortunately, what he thought was love was jealousy on her part of the women waiting in the wings.

The Cosmic Being said to his son, "Because you never went to God to help you see the light. You never prayed to receive the help that you needed because you never believed in God. And you never asked for help. I would have showed you the way to go."

As it stands, the woman who was waiting in the wings to date the Cosmic Being's son was the woman he was supposed to marry. They would have been very happy together, but he didn't do what God wanted him to do. He started to cry and cry. His father said, "You see, this is why we have issues with you on earth. We give everyone choices. You didn't see which way to go even though you have more intelligence than most humans on earth do." The son is extremely bright as a soul and one day will have many blessings to share with others. But since he didn't mature, he lost out in life. The woman moved on. She was the one praying to God. God told her that the man was her man, but he was rebellious and confused and never asked God for help, even though God could have straightened things out between the two. At present, the woman on earth is still not dating anyone, since she loved him very much. The two would have made a great match. She was older than he, but that was not an issue in their relationship.

The Cosmic Being's son has really straightened up and has said, "I wish I could remember on earth what I know now in the Octaves, but that is the secret." All souls on earth are blocked from knowing the answers. They must choose wisely and learn how to make the right decisions on their own. How can a leader become a leader if he does not pass the tests on earth? Earth is the testing ground for developing a wonderful soul. Humans must realize that praying to God is the thing that will answer their questions in life. God will show them what way to go when making life-changing decisions such as getting married, in which state (or region, province, and so forth) to live, for whom they should work, and what type of career they should have. If more souls on earth would silently pray at night before they went to sleep, calling on their Light Body to help them, then they would find their lives turning around. They would pay off any debts one bill at a time. Do this and see how the Angels and your Light Body help you achieve your goals, help you find your perfect match, and help you achieve your dreams for employment. But you must keep your mind on God.

Chapter Four

Now that I have given you some accounts of souls and their lives, I want you to determine if you see yourself in the stories I picked up from the karmic board to show others how and what happens to souls when they fail Earth, as we say in the heavenly world. They flunk Earth! Now, they must go back and repeat the lesson. The second and third time around, the lesson is harder. We give a soul only so many chances before sending it to the ovens.

I want to explain about the ovens. We have fought the evil ones, existed in this universe for thousands upon thousands of years, and had many experiences about which I can't possibly tell you since they happened so long ago. God set up the universes with rules and laws for everyone to follow. One of the rules is to follow God's rules. The Octaves and the angelic kingdom work very closely together. If a crisis arises, then we count on each other. We don't and won't count on a liar or a lazy soul that doesn't want to work to help mankind. Many thousands of years ago, God set up his laws to stop some souls from continuing on with life because they were useless. God couldn't use them for his kingdom. There was no place for them to go. All beings in all universes accept God's hard work, to grow, and help each other in Gods concepts. We all become very dependent on each other when it comes to facing conflict in the heavenly worlds.

As I mentioned before, we are under siege from the evil ones. If we had kept the lazy souls and the souls that were liars, then we couldn't have used them to work for the good of God. When you are under attack, you want everyone from the Octaves to fight and help save your life and others' lives. You don't want them to sit back on their hind-ends and think that they don't have to work or fight for the cause. It's like having a hurt finger on one hand. The hand is basically out of commission until the finger heals and then the hand becomes fully functional again. It is the same in the Octaves and the angelic kingdom. Everyone works. No one lies. If you do lie, then that is an offense against God, which is taken very seriously. On earth, many people lie. This hurts others. Many have gone to prison because others lied about what they did. We treat those offending souls very harshly when they cross over. We don't show them much kindness since we have been fighting the evil ones, who lie to us constantly.

Before we are attacked by the evil ones they will convey a message to us of what they are going to do. In the last five years of battling with them we know not to believe them. We have absolutely no regard for a liar. Lying is very serious offense, even though many on earth lie frequently. No one seems to take offense at people's lies on earth, until the situation becomes serious, when the lie sends someone to court or gets someone murdered or hurt in some other way.

In God's eyes, lying is a serious offense. We show liars no mercy when they cross over and come to the karmic board. We discuss how they were liars throughout their lives on earth life and mention that they didn't have to lie at all. Now, there are some circumstances wherein lying is okay, such as when a soul attempts to save another's life and tells an untruth to make that possible. We do not consider this a lie. I am talking about the person or soul on earth who lies with great frequency. Most everyone knows someone who lies simply because he or she wants to lie. Liars hurt the people they work with, their own families, and everyone in the community when they continue to lie for no other reason than they don't want to tell the truth.

One woman soul lied for many years. We told her over and over that she needed to stop. She pleaded with and yelled and screamed at us at the karmic board. Everyone was in shock that she was not sent to the ovens. She said that she would stop lying,

My Light Body Speaks and Revealing Secrets of Heaven

so we put her down on earth in three very nice lives so she would get the idea that she did not have to lie. She was married and had wonderful children in all three of her lifetimes. She was not in love with any of her husbands. When she came before the karmic board, she told us that she could and would fall in love with a certain man who was a Cosmic Being. When she met this man, she was not in love with any of her past husbands (but she had married them anyway). In all of her lives, she was very nice to people's faces and spoke very softly. But she was a horrible soul. She would reel in a person by being nice, but then she would stab that person in the back. In one of her lives, she had a mother who was very honest and wanted her child to stop lying.

The mother would wash her daughter's mouth out with soap. The child hated her mother. The mother said, "Stop lying, stop being so lazy, and get your homework done." The mother in this life was a Cosmic Being, as was the father. They both worked with this liar's soul, helping her and teaching her. They gave the child a wonderful home life.

In that particular life, the daughter got married and was smiling at everyone in the wedding party. She turned to her mother and said, "Now I can leave your house. I hate you." The mother was floored because she loved her daughter very much. After the daughter was married to the man who was going to teach her not to lie, he failed in his duty because he gave up, realizing that his wife was a liar. He couldn't stand it but couldn't do anything about it, either. When he corrected her in public to make her stop lying, he embarrassed her, so she began to hate him too.

The couple was living on a farm. The woman, a liar, did not speak to her parents much after her wedding. One day, she was fed up with her husband and pushed some bales of hay from the barn's loft in the hopes of hurting him. The bales of hay fell on him. She climbed down from the roof and went into the house. She never called for help. The man would have lived, but his wife wouldn't save him. He died in the field. After she went outside to see if he was dead, which he was, she went to her neighbors' house and told them that she needed help because her husband was lying in the field and she thought he was dead. The neighbors ran and tried to rescue him, but it was too late. The wife had a funeral for him and was smiling inside the entire time, happy to be free of him and happy that she didn't have to be with him anymore. She was calm and cool, still speaking in her soft voice, but she was behaving as a liar. Everyone in the small farm community was sad to see her husband dead by way of a farm accident. But we in the Octaves know that she contrived his death. She continued to live in that farm community. No one ever saw this woman cry over the death of her husband.

Once this soul crossed over and was in the hospital, we talked to her. Eventually, when she got her memory back, her mother and father joined her at the karmic board to go over what she had done to her husband's soul. Her husband was a Cosmic Being. She stood there, untouched by the ordeal. The karmic board said, "We need to see if you can straighten up and repent of your sins. You killed a person on earth and didn't get caught on earth, but you are caught now."

This woman's soul did not react to what we were saying. She was not nervous and said, "I don't care. I don't want to be married to him anymore. I was tired of him telling me that I was a liar and telling the community that I was a liar. I hated him for doing that to me."

The karmic board exploded and told her off and that she was not to lie again. We said, "This is your last chance to go to earth, once we have a body and someone who wants to take responsibility for teaching you not to be lazy and to stop lying."

The soul said, "Okay." Her parents were very upset with her. Many years passed. She was now going to go down to earth and had picked another soul from the Octaves who had two children and was married to a woman in the Octaves. He said that he would try to teach her not to lie. The life was set up. She would meet him, and they would move to a different state. He would finish out his career in the US military and then join the ranks of civilians. He would work for a company, and she would work for a different company. They would have two children in that life.

The couple had a great life, as far as money goes, since the wife never spent much money on clothes. However, she didn't clean house and wasn't a good worker. At her job, she took many opportunities to throw co-workers under the bus.

After some time, the husband, a Cosmic Being, came up to the karmic board and said, "I failed. I can't stop her from lying, and I can't get her to clean the house or boil water because she is so lazy." Her parents also came to the karmic board in tears because their daughter, a soul more than two thousand years old, continued to lie.

We can't have liars in the Octaves. So, the karmic board asked, "Has she improved or gone deeper into her behavior?" The parents said that she hadn't changed and that her current husband was now seeking a divorce. With the children now grown, the husband, a Cosmic Being, was selling the house and asking his wife where she would like to live. He said that he would buy her a townhouse and pay cash so that she wouldn't have a mortgage payment. She could live there for the rest of her life. She was not complying with anything the divorce courts had ordered her to do, and she lied in court when she had to appear. Very upset that she had to go through this, she was nasty to everyone in her home. Now forced to move and get a divorce, she lied to the attorney and judge alike. Both of these men got the hint that this woman was a little off, mentally speaking.

The husband was still going to work. The woman was laid off and then found another job, this one at a church. Her co-workers soon realized that she was under stress because she was crying at work. She told them what she was going through, but she told them nothing but lies. The entire congregation at the church prayed for her since she painted a horrible picture of her husband and her life. She had plenty of money, over half a million dollars, but she told the people at church that she was poor. Her boss excused her for not being at work on time and for not doing her work since she was under stress. She couldn't function. While she left her work undone, the well-off church still paid her a nice salary. Still, the church needed the work done. The other women in the office help her with her work. One day, they surprised her by coming to her front door at home.

They said, "Hi. How is everything? Can we come in? We wanted to bless your house." The woman was in shock. She introduced her co-workers to her family. They saw that her husband, a Cosmic Being, had manners and was a military man. They also met the two grown boys.

When everyone was sitting around, the boys offered the guests something to drink. The scene that these churchwomen saw was totally different from the scene that the woman (who is a liar) had described to them. They all talked, smiled, and joked around during the visit. When the women from church left the $500,000 house in which their co-worker lived, they were in shock, unable to understand what had happened inside the house. They were confused. Back at the church, they talked to the pastor and told him what they saw. What they witnessed, they said, was a family not at odds with each other at all, everyone taking the divorce in stride and talking to each other. The women mentioned that their co-worker lived in a beautiful $500,000 home with a huge $20,000 deck built on the back. They said, "Everything was tidy and there were even antiques—rare finds—in the living room."

The minister said, "Say nothing to her, but be nice and help her. I want to pray to God about this situation and see what we can do to help her." When the minister went into prayer, the women did too. They didn't tell him what they were doing. They wanted an answer from God, as well. One of the women was very aware, could feel others' vibrations, and could get messages from God. She never told anyone about the things she could do, but she used this gift to her advantage. When the minister went into prayer to seek God's face, he prayed about how he could help this woman.

He asked God, "What are we not seeing with this woman? Are we seeing things correctly and doing the right thing?" Once he left the altar, he went back to his office and made some phone calls. Then, he started reading the Bible, wherein he saw the story of a liar. He started to think, *What if everything the woman said was a lie?*

The woman who had gifts similar to the instruments and who could tell when a person was lying sought God's face too. She asked God, "You mean she is a liar?" God said yes. The woman was floored.

When everyone else was at work the next day, the lying woman called and said that she had to take the day off, telling them another lie. They said, "Great. You handle your affairs, and we will take care of your desk." All the workers at the church could now speak freely, since the woman they were praying about was not there. The churchwomen went to the minister.

He said, "I was reading in the Bible where a man was a liar and caused much havoc in his village because he was spreading lies. I had prayed to God at the altar and wanted to know how I could help this woman. The answer came back that she was lying about many things to make others feel sorry about her situation and that she deserved every bit of this divorce since she is the awful one in the marriage." If she had passed the test in that lifetime, then she would have been rewarded with a new husband, one she loved. Also, she would have been blessed with money from the divorce since the Cosmic Being wanted to give her money and a house so that she would be safe. But he was through with her lies. Plus, she hardly ever took a bath.

The Cosmic Being husband said that his tour of duty was over and he would move on and remarry his twin flame, who was on earth, when he met her. This was set up in his profile and in his flame's profile, as well.

The church employees all went back into prayer and sought God's face. They still felt that their co-worker was lying to them, and they wanted to get to the bottom of it. The next day, when the lying soul came to work, they asked her what happened at the court hearing the day before. She started to cry, saying that she had to move out of her house. They asked her, "Are you going to get money from your ex-husband to buy a new home?"

She said, "Yes, he will give that to me."

The minister, very aware and smart, came out and called the woman into his office—rather, a special room attached to his office for private conversations. He told her that he had been praying and praying about her, that he wanted to help her, and that his staff members outside were also praying about her situation. He said that he and the staff came up with the same thing in their prayers. The woman asked, "Really?"

He said, "Yes. We all thought it was time to pray harder, see if we could move mountains for you, and see what we needed to do for you so that you could go on, have a godly life, and be blessed by God."

The woman was shocked! Feeling somewhat fearful, she asked, "What do you mean?"

The minister said, "You know what I mean. I want to make your life better. Sometimes, we must cut the rough stuff from our lives, the stuff that hurts others. We must have operations so that we can take out the bad cells. We can continue to bless and love God when we are upright and healed. When we are over our medical problems, then we are all better. My staff and I have thought long and hard about this. I have a great staff and a great congregation. Everyone in this congregation wants to worship God. They depend on me to give the best sermons I can possibly give to guide and lead them when times are tough. They depend on me to heal them when they hurt. We are all pulling together to become one body, as all members should become one body, just as Christ wants us to do."

The woman was thinking, *what does that mean?*

The minister said, "This means that when we are one body, we are all on the same page, worshipping God and having no other gods before the one true God. We all begin to think alike and work hard together. I noticed that you have not done much of your work. Others are picking up the work and getting it done since the church needs these things done so that I can lead and guide my congregation. I can't have employees who don't do their work. The congregation pays your salary, not me. I don't have any money. I get a salary from my congregation. I need to be honest with them, just as I want you to be honest with me and the entire congregation.

My Light Body Speaks and Revealing Secrets of Heaven

When one seed in the congregation does not fit in, then we must cut it loose. When I was praying to God about you, he told me that you were a liar and that it's not bad that you are getting a divorce. You never loved your husband and made sure not to do the things for him that a wife should do. The man is tired of it. Plus, you have been lying to us for months now about your situation. I don't want to contaminate my congregation. I want them to love each other, but no one can love a liar. So I will give you your final paycheck and wish you the best with your situation. If you want to come to church, you can, but you will not be working for me."

The woman was in shock! She went home and told her husband that she was let go. He said, "Oh, did they find out that you were a liar? That is why they came by the house, to see what was really happening. They saw that you were telling them lies. And no one likes a liar." The woman cried. She went out looking for another job.

The woman was exposed as a liar. We are hoping that by the time she crosses over, she will have stopped lying and changed her behavior.

When you meet one of these lying souls on earth, know that he or she has actually been a liar for thousands of years. We are giving the soul yet another chance to change. If this woman doesn't change, then we will send her to the ovens. She has hurt many people in her many past lives—and she has had many lives. All of the souls that were in contact with this woman were hurt and don't want to share a life with her on earth ever again. When we are attacked, we need help, prayer, and someone to watch our backs while we fight. We don't trust this soul to do these things for us at all.

That is why being a liar is a great, great offense to all of us and why liars usually end up in the ovens. We walk on and say that we tried. We prayed and taught and even spent a lifetime with the soul, but we could not reach it. We see where we might not be able to reach this soul, either. So, for anyone who is reading this book, please remember that lying is a great offense to God. We don't take it lightly. We punish very harshly when a soul lies.

Tell the truth and you will be blessed with a life of happiness and many other lives on earth.

Everyone in the Octaves works to come back to earth since it can be great fun. We give those lives out sparingly now since we are cleansing the earth of evil. This woman soul is evil in our eyes because she lies. She hurts others, and that is evil to us in the Octaves and the angelic kingdom. In the Octaves now, we have decided to grant lives (a body on earth) only to those souls that are balanced and working for God. We are slowly eliminating the evil from earth by doing soul exchanges and granting fewer and fewer lives on earth. The souls now need to explain to the karmic board how they are going to help mankind rather than asking, "What are you going to do for me?" We have changed the concept recently, so it will take many years to change out the many souls who are evil and liars. We are replacing them with honest souls that can do the job of helping mankind on earth.

Call on your Light Body to help the person who is a liar. That Light Body will call on its Light Body to help the person too. Let's see if we can change the world by having everyone call on their Light Body to improve hurtful or negative situations on earth. God wants all souls to learn and grow and not have to face some of the very negative things that are happening on earth. God never ordered these negative things for mankind. As we continue to fight the evil ones, who come nightly with armies of trillions, we will never give up protecting mankind. On behalf of all of mankind, those in the Octaves and the angelic kingdom are fighting for a better life, one that includes the joy and love of God and the happiness that God wants all souls to have.

Chapter Five

In dealing with the evil ones since 2010 and realizing that everyone in the Octaves and the angelic kingdom was living in a cocoon for the past twenty-five thousand years, we, as a group of souls, never dreamed or imagined that some souls would not believe in God and would be against God's laws and would form armies and legions of evil souls to fight the godly souls and try to kill them. As we all quickly began to learn how to fight, we were, for the first time, introduced to the BEING soul of which we had heard. But no BEINGS lived in the Octaves. They have always lived in the other universes. We know about them, but we had never met them. So, that has been a great experience, since the BEINGS had past experiences with the evil ones. Some of the BEINGS that have much light are high enough to be kings of a planet. When their planet was taken from them, everyone escaped. Each one of those souls left for another universe or to find safer ground, from where they could continue to help God's kingdom and defend the younger souls who knew nothing about the evil ones.

Today, we have several hundred thousand BEINGS in the Octaves. They are managing and helping the Octaves, training and teaching us about those things we had never learned and which we need to know because we were inundated with evil ones who joined the army. Before we knew it, more than ten thousand Cosmic Beings had joined the ranks of the evil army. When we found this out, we, of course, annihilated them in the ovens. They seemed proud to go to their deaths when they all stood outside the ovens to say good-bye to their loved ones and friends.

We lived with them for thousands of years, never realizing that they were evil. They pulled us around like puppets on a string, at times. We were ignorant about this group of souls that inhabit every universe. We actually went into shock and could hardly fight them or deal with what they were doing to us. We learned some of their character traits, which include constant lying, laziness to not help the Octaves work for mankind, game-playing, and pretending to be sweet and kind while cutting souls down and killing them. When we saw all of these character flaws, we decided we didn't want these types of souls in our camp anymore. We need souls that believe in God, pray to God, help mankind, and have compassion and love for mankind. As a soul lives on earth, it should develop these wonderful characteristics so that when it makes the ascension, it will have that character. We believe that one can't teach a person to have love, respect, or compassion for another unless that soul experiences certain things on earth when living out many lives by way of reincarnation.

We have all experienced the death of a loved one—in at least one of our lives. And we all have been hurt by a best friend or family member. This teaches us not to nurture the personality traits mentioned above. All of the lives that one experiences should show a soul that it needs to be kind and loving, as well as thoughtful and compassionate about life and God. Many times, mankind doesn't see things this way. People begin to resent God for bringing them to certain experiences. When they ask, "Why did I have to learn this or that lesson?" we say, "To build your thought base. To know what it feels like to have that experience and never do those things to another human being, ever!" Once a soul has a difficult experience, it gains more wisdom, of course. The affected person can, in turn, help the next person on earth who is going through the same thing or something similar. The soul can be a friend to talk to and help the other person along his or her pathway. All of this is designed to build character and subject the soul to the initiations it needs to understand life and ultimately make the ascension. If a soul makes a mistake, this builds the soul's compassion, allowing it to understand the entire situation it went through. When we appoint a soul to the karmic board, it is one that has had many hard lives and experienced difficult things. When the soul comes to the karmic board and has failed in some way in its last life, the karmic board has the reason, compassion, and wisdom to deal with that particular soul, since all members of the karmic board also went through certain situations to learn and grow. This is called a soul's growth. The soul grows by undergoing very difficult initiations on earth, which strengthen the soul's character.

One of the initiations: Loves someone who doesn't love you. This is very difficult because you want the person to love you. Your heart is breaking at the thought that he or she might be with another. You hurt inside for years. This initiation takes about ten years to complete. Souls subjected to this initiation on earth are very high. They can't understand why the other person doesn't like or love them. I am not talking about a marriage situation. I am talking about two people who meet and like each other. We have profiled them to like and love each other so that they can experience the process of loving someone who doesn't love them and thereby grow from it.

One of the individuals in this type of relationship is the rubber band. To explain it as simply as I can, I'll say that the other soul in the relationship pulls and pushes away the person who needs to go through the soul's-growth initiation. As a Light Body, I think that this is one of the hardest lessons that all people need to face. The rejected person's heart breaks. He or she can't seem to get the relationship out of the rubber-band cycle. It continues for about ten years. Initially, the two people meet and get along, but then they separate. And while this is happening, many of these people's friends say, "Stop wishing and dreaming about him [or her] and get on with life." But they haven't seen the profile showing that this person is a high soul and needs to experience loving someone who doesn't return the love for about ten years. This helps the rejected soul develop love for God, which is what the initiation is all about.

At times in a person's life, experiences come across his or her pathway and he or she asks, "Where is God in this situation?" God is always there. The person must continue to have faith in and love for God. All of the initiations are about God and loving him. How can you love God if you don't experience these other situations? How can you continue to believe in God and walk the pathway with him if you don't have these experiences? At the end of this and every other initiation is a rainbow. You must wait on and be patient with God, for God has his own timing.

When all of us in the angelic kingdom and the Octaves were going through the horrific war with the evil ones, every day we uncovered another issue. We put those evil souls into the ovens and began to wonder, *what is God doing with this group of souls?* Up here in the heavenly world, everyone is still growing and learning. Growth and knowledge are not reserved only for people on earth. We in the heavenly world experience these things too. We all began to grow, pray harder, learn how to fight, and learn about the liars and game players. We started to realize that we were very innocent in our thinking and had been living in a cocoon. Our management team changed because the previous one was just as inexperienced as we were. We needed to be taught how to spot the evil beings that were living among us. When the BEINGS came to live with us, we saw that they had so much light around them. Amazed, we asked them, "How come you have this much light?" They laughed at our innocent ways, even though we have great hearts for God. As we began to grow, see more things, and extend the Octaves from Hawaii all the way to England and then down through South America, we built more housing for all the new souls that were coming to live with us, help us, teach us how to fight, and fight with us. When we were attacked, they fought our battles. The original crew ran into a hole that we had dug to protect ourselves, since we never knew how to fight. We were afraid and prayed while down in the hole, one that we had spent weeks digging out so that more than three million Cosmic Beings could fit into it. Down there, we all became very close and realized how innocent we were, living in a cocoon.

I am telling this story because a reader may be going through a very difficult time, as we were five years ago when we learned that there were more than ten thousand evil ones living in our camp. The angelic kingdom experienced the same thing. We began to come together and help each other. The angelic kingdom and the Octaves are usually separate. We do our work and the Angels do their work. The Angels help us in the Octaves by praying for us and healing us, just as we do for all of mankind. While experiencing these life changes, we realized that we needed to change. Of course, it was difficult. Tempers flared. We had arguments and difficult moments since we could hardly fight. We couldn't determine if the evil ones were playing games with us or lying to us. They did nasty things to us, and then we realized that they were evil. At that point, we marched them down to the ovens.

As we grew, we had to take lessons on how to fight and win the battles that the evil ones instigated. They came at us a trillion at a time. At first, it took us two days to fight them and win these battles. We eventually won all battles that went on for a year. Once we noticed how the evil ones operated and handled things, we became more proficient and wise. We put an end to their games and lies sooner than we had previously. When the BEINGS came to join us, we saw that they had gifts that we had never thought of. One of their gifts was radar. They could draw a board in midair, call up a certain person, and track his footsteps to see if he was evil and learn what he was actually doing. We began to rely on the BEINGS to help us. They introduced us to many spiritual gifts. None of us in the cocoon state had any of those gifts. We also found out that there were more than fifteen levels to making the ascension than we realized. We were amazed to find these things out, given that we had never heard of them before. Many on earth, of course, know about making the ascension and becoming one with God. It happens when one's soul and one's I Am Presence mesh together.

This is public knowledge on earth. Those who believe think that they make the ascension and that's it! But, as we found out, that is only the first step on the ladder. One must progress through different levels of making the ascension. As one continues to grow in wisdom, one climbs the ladder of ascension, gaining much wisdom and, along the way, receiving more gifts to use in helping mankind. One's ability to heal, for instance, can become very pronounced. We who have this healing capability can go down to earth and start to heal people who live in areas of strife.

We were all changing as fast as we could while dealing with the evil ones. We eventually got rid of all the evil ones in the Octaves once they were exposed. They can hide their flaws, just as a liar hides the fact that he or she is lying (but when one finally listens to that person, one realizes that he or she tells lies). We were in the same boat since we could hardly see what was happening around us. We didn't have the light, either. We all had about two or three inches, or maybe a foot, of light. As I said before, those who have more light are higher in the pecking order. Given our ranking system in the Octaves, we saw whose light was brighter by looking at their auras. This way, we could determine who the boss was. But since *none* of us had heard about the other levels of the ascension, none of us were really very high. We noticed that the BEINGS had plenty of light, shining like floodlights in a sports stadium when they walked around. We took orders from them. They taught us how to do more things to better help mankind. They pushed us and told us what to do, which stretched our envelope. Those who were not very good at managing were put in other positions. Finally, after five years, we now have a balance in the Octaves and angelic kingdom alike. Those in the angelic kingdom who couldn't manage a group or lead others were replaced with Angels that could do this. The replacement Angels came from other universes and had the experience of leading a group of Angels.

For the last five years, we were stretched, yelled at, and told that we were inept and not very good at our jobs. We began to grow because we didn't want our bosses telling us that we couldn't do the job. We wanted to help mankind but were not doing a good job. We were innocent in our approach, basically living in a cocoon, which damaged us and which was no help to mankind, either. Along with learning a new way of doing things, we gained much wisdom, grew, received more responsibilities, and became happier. We could see the light at the end of the tunnel. We grew so much that we can now talk to our I Am Presence bodies by pulling them out and getting a message from them. This is one of the gifts that we all share now. We are all on either the third or fourth step of the ladder. Now, when the evil ones attack us and unload a huge army on us, we can fight them within a few hours and win the battle. We have never lost one since we were trained how to fight.

We see that mankind has similar experiences. We see where they dislike God and don't want to go through their particular experiences. They begin to rebel, getting nasty and hating God. This is a shame, because one needs God the most when one goes through these experiences. All of us in the heavenly realm are very glad that we went through this experience. We not only saved our own lives but also saved mankind's life. If we had approached the experience with resentment, then maybe none of us would be alive today and I would not be writing this book with the instrument. Those who would have otherwise read this book would not have gained the wisdom in it or realized that we all go through tough times so we can learn many things. I can say, as can all other Light Bodies, that it was horrific at times. Sometimes, we fought for three days straight and were so tired that we could hardly answer prayers. We were fighting on behalf of ourselves and mankind. When you go through tough situations on earth and it's very difficult to understand why you are going through them, know that it's to make you grow, change, and learn something different. Whether it's a love experience, losing your job, losing a loved one, moving to another place and meeting new friends, experiencing new weather patterns, gaining new insights into how others live in the snow, finding what you need to buy for the snowy season—or moving to a hotter area and realizing what you need to live in that part of the country—being told a lie, or being set up, which we all have experienced, you need to look at these things and see where you have changed, what you have learned through that experience.

This gives a soul wisdom. When you cross over, you keep that wisdom and become a candidate to help another person on earth since you have gone through a similar experience. When we had to learn how to strategize for battle, whom do you think we called upon in the Octaves? We called on the military men who have crossed over; they taught us how to strategize and circle the evil ones to win battles. Since then we have won all battles, I am proud to say. The evil ones are very vicious, but we have never given up. Reader, you shouldn't give up, either. Look at your difficult experience with the intention of finding out what you can learn from it.

The instrument had a revelation one day about her dating a certain fellow. He was very nice, but she was not in love with him. She said to God, "I really like his personality, the way he handles money, the fact that he is calm and, at times, funny, and how he handles himself in public." She broke up with the man, however, telling him, "I am not in love with you, but I think you are wonderful." He understood. He wanted to get married but was not in love with her. They remain great friends to this day. The instrument realized that what her former partner brought to the dating scene was something she liked in men. She was sad for several weeks since she was used to seeing him and they had some history together, but she just couldn't go on with him since he wanted to get married and she would not marry a man with whom she was not in love. We want all of mankind to think, "*What did I learn from that experience?*" We want people to incorporate the insight they gain from each experience into their lives and tell others what they learned.

When one of the instrument's girlfriends came to her after breaking up with a nice man whom she missed very much, the instrument said, "Pray to God for a new man who has the same character traits as the last man—only this time, fall in love with him." In this way, she passed on the wisdom she had gained from her experience to another person, who was helped by the conversation.

All of us in the heavenly world are proud to say that we have grown much. When crossovers comment about the heavenly world, saying that it is peaceful, they couldn't be more wrong. We get them out there within a month to help us fight. They are so surprised after they cross over to find that they work harder in the Octaves than they did on earth. Sometimes, they want to go back to earth so they don't have to work so hard and fight the battles that come at us for six to eight hours nonstop every night. As you are driving to work, call on your Light Body and ask it to help you and teach you the things that you seem to have missed in a lesson. Have your Light Body remind you of what you are learning or what you need to show others so that they learn.

All Cosmic Beings are down on earth to teach and help; maybe they have a small lesson to learn too. We sent two Cosmic Beings down to earth recently. One was a doctor who lived in England. His brother went into the military. The two were able to see each other daily. To reach the heavenly world, they left their bodies one night. Each brought the other's earth body to show what it looked like. They met the next day on earth and began to talk. Of course, these two Cosmic Beings are advanced. Most Cosmic Beings can't do such a thing and don't know they are Cosmic Beings until they are about thirty years old. We block out that memory for most everyone who is in an earth body.

Down on earth, the two brothers learned to do their jobs. They met and talked in pubs in England, where they both live. We exchanged their souls because they needed to experience what earth was all about, given that they had not been down on earth for many thousands of years. This time, they wanted to have knowledge of life on earth for about a year. We put them in bodies. Each had a wife and one small child, a girl. They loved children since they have many children in the Octaves. Their children on earth were growing and learning. (Some of the children in the Octaves have made the ascension, so they are working for God. Others are still struggling to get the message.)

The brothers began their travels on earth. They liked to eat. In the Octaves, we don't eat at all. They are now seeing what it is like to be married again and are having a difficult time with their wives' mouths. The daughters, though, are wonderful. The two men put their heads together and said, "This is the time to teach our wives about God and the heavenly world." And so they began to tell stories to their daughters at night while putting them to bed. They told their wives that they were making up the stories.

Each man told his wife the story of what's been happening in the heavenly world for the last five years. The wives didn't believe that such things could happen in the heavens. The men asked them, "What if it can happen and there is really an evil camp?"

The wives asked, "Why doesn't God help them and get rid of the evil ones?"

The men asked, "What if it's to help them grow, fight, and learn the different things they need in order to change the way they operate in the heavenly world?"

The wives asked, "Why would God do that to the spiritual beings?" The answer is because it teaches us through experience. If we are not exposed to earthly things, then how could we in the heavenly world help those down on earth? If we don't know how to count money, be married, endure the pitfalls of being married, and experience being married to the wrong person, then how can we understand human beings?

The wives said, "We are taught in church that God will help you."

The Cosmic Being brothers said, "That is correct, but you must have the motivation to want to change and help yourselves, and then God will send you the pathway and the answer about what to do next—and that helps you. God will not fight your battles, but God will send you the answers and the way to fight your battles so you use godly wisdom. In using godly wisdom, you learn how God works in your life."

The wives asked, "Then what?"

The Cosmic Beings said, "Then, you can count on God to get you through all your trials and tribulations. You become a believer, thinking that since he got you through the other experiences; he will get you through this one. And you will be more apt to believe and continue to call on God when the next experience comes along, because after each hard experience, we receive a blessing. God shows us that pathway too."

The instrument has had a hard life. Many things saddened or upset her, but here she is today, still believing in God. Now we are having her write books by doing automatic writing, where she can hear us speak to her all day long, which is a gift. She is typing what I am saying to her because, after passing all her initiations and experiencing losses, she is now ready for a blessing. This blessing is providing the world with books to read so that readers can then help the next person or soul in their path. The instrument is now happy to know that God is on his throne and takes care of his own. Of course, the instrument was surprised to find out that she would be writing books for the public. She said, "I can't write a book." But, as you can see, this is her first book on the market. She has written four others that were not dictated and will publish in the near future. We will send those books forth too so that others can gain insight from them and develop the wisdom to tell others what the heavenly world is really all about.

The two Cosmic Beings in England did a soul exchange and learned many things. When the wives cross over, the brothers will be the first ones there to greet them. The two women will say, "Thank you for teaching me the many things that I was doing wrong and what was wrong with my personality." They both are very grateful for that experience of taking a good, hard look at themselves and changing the character flaw they never realized they had. Today, they are regarded as wonderful Cosmic Beings who brought that wisdom back. They now help their children on earth with financing, investments, balancing checkbooks. They point out to their children on earth what they need to do to gain happiness and joy from a life on earth. All Cosmic Beings visit their children on earth and help them with the situations they face. If they can't reach them, then we in the Octaves do a soul exchange and replace the body with a Cosmic Being. We train and teach that soul, showing it what it was doing wrong on earth and how it must change to become the great soul that God wants all souls to become.

Chapter Six

Now that I have explained how the godly world works, you can see that all the experiences you have while living on earth can be of benefit to you as you search your heart and mind to find the common denominator among everything that you have learned. And, also determine what you can take with you on your life's journey. As I have explained, we all learn and grow. You take any wisdom gained with you as you go. Your inner light expands within and you are much higher up on the stepladder of growth. You become the big fish in the pond giving orders all day long, rather than the little fish in the pond taking orders all day long.

This is where I explain to all those in the angelic kingdom that just because, for example, you were a vice president on earth doesn't mean that you are that highly ranked in the heavenly world. We, of course, process over a thousand crossovers daily. Coming from all walks of life, they are usually glad to have arrived. I know that when someone dies, he or she leaves saddened loved ones behind. But for the most part, the crossovers are glad that life is over. When they cross over in their senior years, it is because they have actually asked to cross over. We make sure, before a Cosmic Being or Angel crosses over, that he or she has completed his or her mission on earth.

When a person says to a friend or family member, "I am ready to leave, I've had a good life," he or she actually means it. We work on that person's behalf to ensure that he or she makes the transition. In general, older people know that they have done their jobs for God while on earth, have blessed whom they were supposed to bless, and have finished the task at hand. When they cross over, many say, "I didn't think God was listening to my prayers." But God is always listening to everyone's prayers. If you want to cross over but still have things to accomplish, then we keep you on earth so that you can enjoy what you are doing.

There is nothing to fear about crossing over. It's very peaceful and calm. You are bathed in love and light. All the doctors and nurses who work in the hospital are very compassionate. They have had very hard lives, as I have said before, which allows them to have compassion for others. Our doctors are trained for more than ten years to learn what they need to learn about our bodies, which are different from earth bodies. We describe them as being of semi-hard consistency—like Jell-O. They can be cut and burn like human bodies. We can also get diseases, for instance if we were on a dying planet. The toxic gases coming from that dying planet could erode our bodies. Those who endure this must remain in the hospital for months before they are well enough to leave. Our hospital is huge, about five football fields in size. Many come to the hospital with some type of illness since they were out traveling around in other universes. They come here to be treated because our hospital is known for being one of the best in all of the universes.

As the new students trains to become a doctor, they take classes and work alongside the medical staff who are training them in what they need to do while attending to a patient which is call practical application. They continue to study their medical books, and work alongside the doctors for hands on application. They study their books and also have practical application. They also treat patients, giving shots and administering medication under the supervision of the doctor who is guiding them. They are graded in that aspect and also on their written and oral exams. When a rare surgery is scheduled, the doctors invite the students into the operating room to teach them how to perform the surgery. One of our doctors is a specialist. In fact, all doctors in our hospital are specialists and can perform surgery on all parts of the non-human body.

As we in the heavenly world seek marriage, we must date someone for over three hundred years before marrying for life. The two individuals in question must work alongside each other and do many things together except live with each other and have sexual relations together, because these things are against God's laws. Our species is different, which is something that most humans don't know. A Cosmic Being's body and sex organs are different from the bodies and sex organs of BEINGS and Angels. If a BEING and an Angel want to get married, they can, since they have the requisite complementary sex organs. But if an Angel and a Cosmic Being want to get married, then the male must go into the operating room and submit to surgery to make him able to have sex with the Angel. So many times, Angels and Cosmic Beings become great friends but don't marry. Whereas, once they were married on earth, they cross over to find out that the woman is an Angel and her husband on earth was a Cosmic Being. They usually don't marry, but there are times when the Cosmic Being man does have the operation on his sex organs. Once he goes through that, he can't go back to being a Cosmic Being. He is now an Angel.

All Angels' bodies are designed like the human body, and Angels have sex the same way that humans do on earth. But the Cosmic Being doesn't have sex in the same way. I will not go into details. I am mentioning this to give the reader a better understanding of heaven, as we don't usually have the opportunity to have a gifted instrument hear what we say and accept it. Even though there are many on earth who can hear spirits talking to them, people are not apt to believe in the spiritual realm. When they cross over, we ask them, "What happened to you? Why didn't you want to tell the world about us and help us?" They say they didn't want to be looked upon as crazy. Because of that, they refused to write books or talk at conferences to tell humans what to expect when they cross over.

When the BEINGS came to the Octaves five years ago to help us fight the evil ones, everyone knew that BEINGS and Cosmic Beings could never marry because they couldn't change their sex organs to complement each other's. Since they will never be married, they don't entertain the idea. They all live very well with each other and fully understand that they will never marry. It's fruitless for them to entertain the idea. Angels and BEINGS, however, can marry. When they produce a child, the child is an extremely beautiful and highly intelligent soul that usually ends up ruling planets, given the beauty of the Angel. This is not to say that BEINGS are not just as handsome, but the combination of the two parents' genetic material produces a stunning effect in the offspring. The Queen of Queens is one such soul. Her father was a BEING with dark hair. He was very tall and had chiseled features and piercing dark eyes. The mother was an Angel. All Angels, when you see them, are beautiful. They have strong bodies and either dark or golden hair. Very smart, they move in a quiet manner and go about their work very thoughtfully. The Queen of Queens is a combination of this parental mix. She is stunningly beautiful. None of us can put into words how gorgeous she is, as I said before, she has curly blonde hair and piercing blue eyes.

Marriage on this side is not without its downfalls, either. Some couples, after fifty thousand years of marriage, are not in love anymore and want out of the marriage. They go into the hospital and have a separation operation, which involves taking the etheric body's webbing, pulling it back from both bodies at the same time, and then replacing the webbing into each one of the souls on the operating table. This is how they are divorced. They have to stay in the hospital for approximately two months to heal. And then they go about their lives separately. Since we don't have money up here, there is nothing for them to do other than live apart and go back to the jobs they once had, if they so choose. Or they can move on to another job in the Octaves. We train all souls in the Octaves for many different kinds of jobs so that they have well-rounded experience in all the things that need to be done for mankind. As the crossovers enter the octaves, some soul exchanges come back to the Octaves because they failed to follow God's orders. At the karmic board when we discuss with the soul who is about to take a soul exchange position instead of coming in a birth.

We explain in full detail why the other soul failed to do God's work in that life and we are conducting a soul exchange to see if we can still achieve God's will in that particular person's body. As I the Light Body explains in the next story about two women who failed in their life to do God's will in their life.

Two women, friends on earth, were happy not believing in God. They thought that those who did believe in the Christ or God were nuts! The first woman I'll tell you about was facing a divorce. She was in shock that her husband of ten years was divorcing her. She thought about the week before, when she told her girlfriends that she had a great marriage. The following week, her husband told her that he was leaving and would buy another house for himself. His wife, he said, could have the townhouse since she could afford it. The wife cried. Her girlfriends came to her aid. The husband got sick; he was now dying of cancer. He wanted none of his wife's help. He moved in with his family in another state and had to sell his new house. The wife called and asked, "How are you doing?"

He said, "I am fine," knowing that it was just a matter of time before he left earth.

His wife said, "Do you want me to help you with the money and investments?"

He said, "I have it all taken care of. Thank you."

She cried and cried; in shock that he didn't like her anymore. One day, she asked him, "What happened to us?"

He said, "I couldn't stand your mouth. It was harsh. You would yell and scream at me, while on the streets you were this little angel whom everyone thought was so nice. I know different. Take it from me: Make sure you don't treat the next man like you treated me."

The woman took that to heart. Her siblings were distant from her too so she began to put two and two together and started to change her life. If her husband had told her earlier in the marriage about her mouth, then I bet the woman would have changed her behavior sooner.

A woman in her sixties was getting married to her ex-husband. They had met when they were in high school and married sometime later. After they divorced, they rekindled their relationship and remarried each other when they were in their sixties. The wife moved to another state to be with her husband and set up the household. The problems started to come in like a tidal wave.

The second woman that I'll tell you about was miserable. Her Cosmic Being father called her up to the Octaves and explained to her that she was lazy. "We need you to work and get the house cleaned up. Actually paint the rooms and get the garbage picked up. Your husband has a bad back and can't do those things. This is your initiation, to work for him, help him (your fellow soul), and also pass the test by not being lazy. You were laid off from every job you ever held on earth." So the daughter went to her divorced girlfriend, complaining and crying because she had to do these things. She was tired and didn't want to do the job. She was sorry that she married this man. Although she did love him, her love was waning very quickly.

Both of these women souls are now trying to learn. They hated their lives, so we did soul exchanges on them. We made them two adorable little girls in a Latin American family. They became unhappy because the mother in the family was crazy. The father didn't know this about his wife. Each day when he came home from work, she seemed fine to him. But the children, if not in day care or kindergarten, were mistreated and told to stay in their rooms all day long. We realized that the girls would never learn about God in this situation, so we crossed them over not long ago.

The girlfriends met in the hospital. They were in shock, asking, "Where are we?" We told them that they crossed over by way of a soul exchange and said that we would have their parents come by in about three weeks to meet them again, once they had a full memory of all their past lives. The girls were in shock! They asked, "What happened to the lives we were living on earth?"

We told them, "Since you did not believe in God and your second family had a crazy soul for a mother, one who couldn't teach you about God, we decided to start you two over fresh. We had you come back to home base so your family could instill in you the value of believing in God."

The girls looked at each other. In three weeks, their parents came to the ends of their beds to meet, greet, and talk to them. The girls were still in shock. They asked, "Are we in heaven?"

We answered, "Yes, in the hospital—and soon you will be moved to your parents' home and live with them."

They said, "No, we don't want to live with our parents." We told them that this is the rule in the Octaves. All children live with their parents until they are married, and it's the parents' responsibility to teach the children about God, teach them to work hard, and demonstrate and demand godly behavior. The look on these two women's faces was priceless when we introduced them to their Light Bodies.

When they adjusted to life in the Octaves, we sent them to the karmic board. They stood there and watched the screen, which was showing a time on earth when they had made fun of a girlfriend. This girlfriend had some spiritual gifts and was educating them about God. Each time (after they saw their friend), the two women went to their houses, spoke on the phone together, and laughed hysterically about what their spiritual girlfriend had to say about heaven. They found it funny that she was talking about twin flames, saying that souls in the heavenly world get married and their called Twin Flames. She said that they had children, which means they have sex. The two friends were hysterical over this comment. They laughed about it for weeks.

They invited this woman out to have dinner with them. She thought that her two girlfriends liked and loved her, but really they just wanted to ask her more questions, holding their laughter in until they said good-bye at the restaurant. After parting ways with her, they began to laugh hysterically at what she tried to teach them about heaven while at dinner.

Once these two souls were in heaven and met their real families for the first time, they could hardly speak because they were in shock. One of the fathers said to his daughter, "Why are you so in shock?" She told him the story mentioned above. The father started to laugh and said, "The joke is on you. The woman at whom you were laughing is also my daughter. She is your sister. You are friends and worked together at one time, but you two never knew that you were sisters in the Octaves." The daughter, still in shock, couldn't speak at all. The father said to her, "There are many things that you and your friend will learn up here, since you two never believed in God in your lifetimes. I wanted you to believe in God. You went to church at times, but you never really believed in God or asked God to help you with your situations on earth. It is true that we get married in the Octaves and are called twin flames thereafter. We do have sex with our partners only, and we are prohibited from sleeping around if not married. You will be living with me and your other brothers and sisters."

The girls looked at each other and asked, "Is this where we pinch ourselves and awake to see that this was only a nightmare?" Everyone roared over their comment.

The father said, "You can pinch yourself all you want. You are in the heavenly world, within the Octaves. It's not a nightmare!"

The two stared at their families. Their mouths dropped open. One said, "This is a nightmare! Where do I get out?" Everyone was roaring so hard at them, but they were serious about leaving.

The father said, "You can't leave unless you can prove to the karmic board that you have something to give to mankind and that you are willing to work very hard to give back to the human race. You must offer mankind a gift, like kindness or joy, or you must provide happiness and serve mankind by way of deeds or profession. That is the only way you will return to earth. You will be trained to believe in and pray to God on a constant basis, and that will change your outlook from nightmarish to peacefully calm. You must learn to change your behavior and not be lazy. All things are possible with God."

The girls, staring at the father, said, "We can't believe it!"

The father said, "Believe it. You are here, and I will guide you two to a better understanding of God. The parents rule the children according to the law of the Octaves. You will live with me and abide by my rules. You will work and you will pray. You

Linda Prior

will help mankind and heal people in all hospitals when you are ready to take on your first assignment." And with that, the parents walked away and left the two girls to think.

Eventually, their memories returned. They remembered their parents and their girlfriend from the earth experience, the one who tried to tell them the truth but whom they didn't believe. Now, they were living the experience.

One day, the two asked the father, "Can we see our girlfriend?"

He said, "No. She is busy serving mankind at this time, but when we do a soul exchange on her, you can tell her that you're sorry for making fun of her behind her back when she was telling you the truth.

"Just because you don't believe it doesn't mean that it's not so."

That is another reason why I am writing this book: to explain many things to the average person, help people with their behavior, and teach them to call on their I Am Presence or Light Body to help them through the rough spots of life. We also wish to celebrate the highlights of life with them. Once the souls on earth pass the hard lessons, the world becomes open. Many blessings are bestowed on the soul that has passed the initiations.

Now indoctrinated into the Octaves, the two girls have met their brothers and sisters. One of the brothers worked at the corporation where the sister worked. She is still in shock that all of these things are connected together. You see, all souls are connected to each other. This is why the sister who crossed over via a soul exchange knew that she had a sister in the Octaves. The brother who was working in the same corporation had a soul exchange too since he didn't call on or believe in God.

The two girls are adjusting to their new life. They take directions from their father and participate in life. They have met their other two sisters, whom they never met on earth, and they are all finally talking to each other and realizing that life is not so bad in the Octaves. But since they had more freedom on earth, they want to go back. They must prove that they can give back to, rather than take from, mankind. They are working very hard to learn and keep learning. Because they don't have light and neither has made the ascension, they take many orders and are very busy. Remember, they are the lowest souls in the Octaves. They will grow and learn and will realize that being the lowest person on the ladder is no fun. They will realize that wisdom is everything in this world called the Octaves.

Now, both girls are living what they never believed was possible. Their girlfriend had told them the truth, but they howled about it behind her back. The laugh is on them. Many times, people hear things about a spiritual person and make fun of him or her at the dinner table or ridicule that person in the privacy of their own homes. They laugh about it, wondering, *how can people believe the rotgut stuff that this person is saying?*

We Light Bodies give every human on earth lessons so that people will change their attitudes about what goes on in the heavenly world. When these people cross over, they are hit, like the two girls were, with such a surprise when they learn that we did a soul exchange on them. They want to pinch themselves and wake up from what they think is a nightmare. We all laugh. But this is exactly what happens to those who don't believe while they are on earth. They don't believe that there is life after death, that Cosmic Beings are their neighbors, and that Angels appear on earth to help mankind, showing them to be as kind to others as the Angels are to them.

One problem that we have with humans is that they don't want to see the signs and change. Some do, but most don't. For example, when someone is fired or laid off from a job, there is usually a reason for it. The reason may be that it is time for that person to change professions or move to another state so he or she can take a job in a different corporation where he or she will be respected. Some people are laid off because they need to find out what is wrong with them. They must do a soul search. One of the souls I mentioned previously was laid off from every job she held. Why didn't she look into the reason and change herself? And that is what we ask ourselves when we are dealing with mankind. "Why can't they see the issues they have in their lives?" The soul who is going over her life with her father is now answering for why she didn't work hard or want to keep her jobs. She's discovering why she became lazy.

Laziness is a serious offense to God. We in the Octaves can't use lazy souls. Reader, know that lazy people have a hard road ahead, as they will be kept up here for many years, working very hard and taking orders to become disciplined and become team players—as we all are team players on the road to godliness. The two worst offenses to God are laziness and dishonesty. Exhibiting these two things will earn you a fast trip to the ovens. We work with the souls, but we also warn them: "This is what you have to do to change." We give them many chances, but, still, the day comes when the soul is on the way to the oven and the parents cry, asking for another chance.

One such soul was the sister of a Cosmic Being. She and he had a life together until she lied about him and he ended up in jail because of it. When they both finished out that life and crossed over, the brother told his sister off. He yelled very loudly because she lied and, as a result, he was thrown in jail—when he was supposed to do something very important in that life. He missed his chance because of her. They moved forward. The sister went down for another life, but the brother refused to go. She experienced a thing similar to what she had put her brother through. Someone lied to her, and she ended up in jail for a few years in one of her lives since she had done the same thing in a past life with her brother. Over the course of a thousand years, this soul, continued to lie. She has had many other lives, and we tried to correct her behavior many times, but she continues lying simply because she can.

In one of her lives, this woman was in an okay marriage. She had two children and was enduring her life while dreaming of someone else whom she wished she had married. She was not attracted to her husband at all. When he told her what he wanted for dinner, she rebelled, unable to withstand anyone's telling her what to do. Everyone in the Octaves and in the angelic kingdom take directions. We all take orders, no matter where we are in the pecking order, whether on the lowest rung of the ladder or the highest. The highest among us, the ones who rule a planet or universe, takes orders from God. We all know that those above us have more light than we do and, therefore, we are going to take orders. Everyone laughs because we all say that we are taking orders.

This woman soul finished out her life and crossed over. Her brother told her that this was the end of the road. She was thrown into an oven because she spent over twenty-five thousand years not doing what God wanted her to do. Before she died, she said, "Let me have one more chance. I will do it this time. I thought you were kidding and that I would never go to the ovens." But we put her into the oven, and that was it. It took us twenty-five thousand years to finally get to the point where we realized that we needed to do something different with this soul.

We are still fighting the evil ones. They constantly lie to us, as they did recently; telling us that they would be moving to the First World called Space and would not attack us anymore. They have come at us since making that comment. Every day, they attack us. We have *no* patience for liars after what we have gone through with the evil ones in the Octaves. At one time, the evil ones even infiltrated the angelic kingdom. Some of them made up part of the leadership. We didn't know they were there until the Queen finally saw them, after which point they were annihilated. Between the Octaves and the angelic kingdom is a distance of about five thousand miles. Between the Astro-World which is an area, that has been used to house souls that were suddenly taken from earth. The soul becomes in shock until it can navigate itself to the Octaves; where once again, the soul is hospitalized until the soul has complete memory of who they are once again. And, the Octaves is a distance of approximately five thousand miles. The highest level of the heavenly world is about thirty thousand miles high. I am assuming, since we don't actually know how many miles. We can guess, but we have never measured it. Between each of these heavenly worlds are many, many miles, so the leaders could hide from us for years and years in the vast sky. But we finally caught them, and they are annihilated. We were told that the leaders' offspring will come after us when they have enough light. Upon hearing this, the Queen laughed and said, "Come to Mama!" Since the Queen of Queens is the highest soul in all the universes and her aura is Six hundred thousand miles wide as I mentioned before. She is not fearful; in fact, she welcomes them, telling us, that it's an opportunity for to annihilate evil once again. The offspring are not here with us, where they could be growing. We don't want evil BEINGS to continue growing in the universes and attacking innocent souls.

After experiencing all of this turbulence, we realized that giving liars multiple chances has not worked in our world. We needed to change and make the changes immediately. On earth, it sometimes takes years to change laws for the benefit of mankind. In the heavenly world, if we need to change processes, as if we worked in a corporation, if the prayer-line is awkward then we change the entire system to function quickly and more efficient - then we change immediately—and that is it. We don't hash it out. We make the necessary change, whether it's instituting a new law or reconfiguring the process for sending souls down to earth. We change processes immediately in the Octaves to make things work more smoothly. Since all life is about growth in the Octaves whatever, a soul desires to benefit his or her growth, is incorporated into the Octaves. Additional classes, training on earth to learn how to heal those in the hospital, answering pray, all is instituted into our daily life in the Octaves and in the Angelic kingdom so all can become great souls and keep its wisdom. Before we send a soul down to earth, that soul must promise the karmic board that it will do something for mankind, not expect us to do something for the soul. As a result, bodies are becoming harder to find. By soul exchange is sometimes the only way a soul can come to earth, work off its karma and try to bless the people who are put in its path. So many souls, when they cross over, have the same reaction as the daughter of the Cosmic Being had: "Am I having a nightmare?" They want to know why they didn't know this information on earth.

We tell them, "We write books and have individuals speak to Angels or Cosmic Beings, but not many believe them."

The other night, the instrument, wanting to finish this book, said, "Let's get this done. The evil ones have been fighting nonstop. I don't want them to hear about this book at this time because they don't want the truth to become available to mankind." So, the other day, when we started on the book, she typed what I dictated to her for more than four hours. We are on the sixth chapter and have a few chapters to go. She awakes in the middle of the night and types another chapter so that the humans on earth can read the truth sooner. Her workplace is an hour away, so she arises at 3:30 in the morning to drive to work. We have limited time to create a book, so we are doing it in one weekend. The instrument doesn't have the leisure of typing whenever she wants to.

Call on your Light Body and ask for guidance about your behavior, stop arguing and fighting with your spouse. Pay off your debts. Find other ways to relax instead of shopping. Save money if you can. Work hard at your job. When the time comes for you to move on, we will tell you to update your resume and post it out on the Internet for headhunters to see. If you were a good worker at your last job, then you will be rewarded with a new job. Those who are lazy at work and want to move on and be blessed with another job are not going to find another job because of their laziness at work. That is the way it works.

The instrument once had a boss who was very detail-minded and asked for many things. The instrument did everything for this boss with a smile. Working more than ten hours a day for this boss, she kept smiling and didn't complain, except to us. She said that the boss was very unfair with the employees. Others on the team were complaining about this boss too. So, the instrument found an opening with another company. She put in her resignation letter and thanked everyone. The boss was in shock once she learned that the instrument was leaving. She had no idea why? The instrument laughed and had fun on the job. Happy with her fellow team members, she was also very pleasant and nice to her boss, who was a micromanager. The instrument did everything required of her. The boss asked for things like, "Did this project get done?" when dealing with all the things she hoped to micromanage. When review time came, the boss made a small but untrue comment about the instrument. The boss said that she would still give the instrument a raise.

The instrument said, "This is untrue, so I will not sign my review." The boss was in shock. "I don't sign things that have lies written about me. I could sue you for defamation of character." The boss was taken aback by the instrument's comment.

When the instrument's resignation letter was on the boss's desk, the boss thought for a few moments and said, "I didn't realize you were unhappy."

The instrument said, "I was not unhappy until you wrote a lie on my review. I worked very hard for you, sometimes twelve hours a day. On Friday nights, we would walk out of the office together at 8:00 p.m. when everyone else had gone by 4:30 p.m. For you to make that comment about me was unfair and uncalled for. It was a lie."

The boss said, "Well, we do that in this company so we don't have to raise a person's salary. That is the way we keep our expenses down on salaries and head count."

The instrument said, "That is karma. It will come back to you and this company." Many companies can't afford to raise everyone's salary, but they do give their employees a cost-of-living raise and never write lies on any employee's review. At the instrument's workplace, after she turned in her letter of resignation, a memo from the CEO and HR department was issued to explain the situation, saying that employee reviews were handled correctly and honestly. It said that reviews help employees and are meant to compliment an employee's performance, not to be unfair. The instrument read the memo as a justification for lying about employees so that they would only get so much of a raise. The instrument thought it was evidence of stupidity, so she left that position to move on.

The boss, to this day, remains very sorry about her actions. She loved the instrument. They made a great team and shared many laughs about many experiences at that company. But the way the boss went about the review earned her some karma. She will pay for that karma. She is of the belief that there is nothing up in heaven, that when you die, you go into the ground and that is it. But when she comes up, she will have an instant reaction to something she finds nightmarish: "Pinch me. Am I dreaming, or am I having a nightmare?" We up here all think that is so funny, because no one is dreaming. It's real.

Chapter Seven

There are millions of Light Bodies in the Octaves and the angelic kingdom. We are all waiting for mankind to call on us. This book will finally tell the truth about Light Bodies, a new concept to mankind. A book has never been written about a Light Body. I can see the late-night TV comedians making derisive comments about Light Bodies, but don't be fooled. We are here and are ready to help you, so call on us and tell us what you want in your life, what you want us to take care of, how can we help you? How you can change. We will help you daily, just as I help my instrument in her daily life. She and I are writing this book together. She goes back to read what I have said after she types it.

All Light Bodies have made several ascensions, so they are very high souls. You can't have a job as a Light Body if you don't pass the many tests or make the many levels of ascension. We are very proficient in our work, helping all souls, including answering prayers and helping to change negative situations in people's homes. If you happen to have a long commute, as the instrument does, then talk to God while you are driving to and from work. Call on your Light Body and begin to talk to him or her about all the things that are on your plate: your workload, your nasty boss, and the job you dislike. A Light Body can handle all of those things. It doesn't happen instantaneously, though; it takes a few weeks for some things and a few months for other things, depending on your karma. Once you overcome your karma, you will reap the blessings. Sometimes, a horrible boss is part of your karma for a while. When you pass the test by being nice to him and continuing to do your job, the horribleness rolls off your back—and then you can change jobs. Many bosses make karma in this life. When they come back in another body, they will have a boss who is the same as they were in their previous lifetime. So, remember to smile, get the job done, and move forward. Don't let it upset you, Know that it's part of life and that you will eventually move on and be blessed. When you are going through this type of difficult situation, the Light Body will put into your aura things that you need to remember, change, or do. That is where you will be helped. When you do the things that you are charged with doing, the situation will become better and you will eventually see the light at the end of the tunnel. Most everyone has had an awful boss. Those who pass the test in that situation are the ones who do the work and don't cause any aggravation in the workplace. Act as if the things at work don't bother you. Don't say much. Just do your work the best you can. When you complain to your Light Body and say that you want the situation to change, the Light Body will go into full work mode, moving mountains to get you to a happier place.

Many souls on earth could use a helping hand. Sometimes, their families and friends don't have an answer for them. If they do have the answers, people sometimes are unwilling to listen to or take advice from those particular individuals because they resent it. They don't want a friend to help them because they would feel inferior if they took the friend's advice.

Say that a person went to college and believes that he or she is brighter than the average person on earth, especially his or her friends and family members. The person would not say such a thing to anyone, but that is the way he or she feels at times.

When a Light Body is called up, he or she assesses the supplicant's situation and looks into the person's aura to call up all of his or her thoughts and see what the bother is, the things that the person doesn't say aloud, even to his or her closest friend. A Light Body can help the person start to clear the ugly thought-forms from his or her aura and reveal to the person that sunshine is on its way, once the aura is cleared and things improve. When people brood over the same negative thoughts for months or years, the negative thoughts cloud around the aura. People find themselves downtrodden with stress and unhappiness. Nothing seems bright for them. They become certain that the future will be horrible, so they become depressed, continuing to think on negative things. Before they know it, they feel the weight of the world on their shoulders or feel certain that they are the only ones who have these problems. They are too proud to ask for help, perhaps by seeing a psychologist and getting some guidance from someone who is neither in their immediate family nor one of their friends. Therefore, they continue to listen to their own negative thoughts which have long-lasting effects.

They can become sick with disease from thinking negative thoughts and never seeing the sunny side of life. They can become rude or nasty to others. They change but don't know that they have changed. They stay at home or shop more. In any event, it's a downward spiral for that individual.

Calling on one's Light Body means that help is on the way. The Light Body can clean a person's aura so he or she can begin to feel better and sleep again. The person who was a shut-in because of depression can once again become motivated to get out and see a friend or walk around the block.

Skin irritations are a symptom of negative thinking. Many people have skin eruptions. The main cause of skin ailments is the type of thinking that produces stress or irritation.

We sent a soul down to earth to be raised by a teacher. Her father was basically a day laborer who worked odd shifts, so the mother was home with the children. She was the schoolteacher. Her mother, one of the grandmothers in this family, was very strict and had raised her children by disciplining them. They had supper, as it was called, at a certain time every night. The children had chores to do on the weekends and studied during the week, they had to do the dishes at night and the basic environment was inflexible and sometimes harsh. The mother raised her three daughters in the same way. She disciplined them when they acted out or had what she called a big mouth. When the girls back-talked the mother, the mother washed their mouths out with soap. As the girls were growing up, two of them didn't get along.

They often fought and were put on restriction when their mother found out about it. The older daughter wanted things her own way. She was very stubborn. Her parents tried to teach her to give in a little, and then she'd see that things would go more her way—when the time came. But this daughter was not willing to give in to anyone. She wanted it her own way. When she was with her family, she was horrid. Later in life, when she was with her friends at college, she was wonderful. Everyone loved her.

Once the two other daughters got married, it was evident that they too had a stubborn streak. They saw themselves in their older sister. They mocked their older sister for being stubborn, but their husbands both complained that *they* were stubborn and wouldn't ever budge.

As they developed, the two younger sisters learned to give in. The older sister—unmarried and in her mid-thirties—is still very stubborn. She is that way at work. She tells someone to do something and, in a hateful voice, says that she wants it done now. All the employees wonder, *"What happened to the boss?" "She used to be so nice."* The woman is now living by herself and wants to sell her house. Wanting to do many things with her life, she can't seem to get past the fact that there are certain rules on earth. You must do certain things or else, if you do them your own way, instead of the spiritual way, you fail to reap the rewards. She had bought a high-end condo years ago. Now, she wants to sell the condo but can't unless she goes about painting it, fixing it up, and repairing all the appliances and leaky faucets. She doesn't want to paint it since she likes the orange walls, but it is hard to sell a home with orange walls unless they were done by an interior designer. When she bought the condo, she borrowed money from her father and said at that time, "I will pay you back when I sell the condo and make money on it." The realtor offered her an interest-only loan for financing and arranged to place a second mortgage on the condo. The woman said, "That is great." Her parents came to co-sign the papers. The realtor smiled because she was selling a property for which she would get a high commission, but she never once explained to her client, one of her girlfriends for more than twenty years, that this loan arrangement would not be in her best interests.

Years later, when many owners around the woman were selling their condos, she asked them, "What did you do?" They said that they moved out all of the unnecessary furniture and put it in storage. They painted the walls, fixed all the faucets, and made sure that all appliances worked properly. They had the furnace and the air-conditioner checked and also made sure that the carpets were cleaned - or they updated the floors to sell the condominium. When this soul was dreaming of selling her condo, she said, "I am not going to do that." She signed a contract at the karmic board thirty five years ago, promising God that she would write spiritual poetry and help God lead people to become spiritual. But she has done nothing since the Mid-thirties, she has been on earth. She has a rare gift for writing poetry. In many of her other lives, she believed in God and was very spiritual.

When we see this soul, we wonder, *what happened?* We see that the stubbornness she was allowed to practice as a child is still with her—and it's more pronounced than ever before. When she lived with her family, they tried to correct her behavior, but now they can't say much since she is a grown woman. This soul had a soul exchange. We thought that putting another soul in her body would help her with the task of writing spiritual poetry for mankind, as she promised God she would do. So, with a second soul in her body, nothing is happening. This soul finds that wine is the answer to everything in her life. She has since become an alcoholic. She takes all of her girlfriends with her to go drinking. They have a great time going to wineries after she asks, "Come with me to the winery?" Her girlfriends realize that this is all she wants to do. Also, she stays pinned up in her condo for weeks, apart from going to work. When she comes out of the condo to do a little bit of grocery shopping, she is tired-looking and heavier than before. Her parents are around and try to help her since they love her very much. We look at this soul and see that she is depressed.

Worried about her, we want her to have a wonderful life, the one that we promised her, but her life is anything but wonderful.

At this time, she has a face full of pimples. She went to every dermatologist in the area. For a while the condition would clear up, only to reemerge and be worse than the last time. She has purple-looking skin and wears very thick makeup to hide the scarring and discoloration.

When she spoke with others about what she needed to do to sell her condo, they asked her, "What type of loan do you have?"

She said, "An interest-only loan. I pay [X] amount of money every month, but my balance has only gone down a little bit even though I am paying on my principal from the second mortgage." These people explained to her what happened with this loan and said that she needed to see a financial advisor and have that advisor get her a better loan. Then, they said, the balance would go down on the condo and she would be able to sell it and move on. While she heard this information, she remains stubborn and wants it done her way. She doesn't want to refinance. She wants to sell the condo and then have the money that she owes on it be placed on the balance of the loan for the new home she will eventually buy. When she says this, people look at her as if she is nuts.

People tell her, "You have the money in your 401K. Take the extra money out of the account and use it to pay off the condo at settlement." Well, she doesn't want to do that either.

One of her friends said, "You will stay in this condo if you don't want to do what it takes to get rid of it."

This woman is very stubborn. If she called on her Light Body and asked for help, the Light Body would make it very clear that she should move on. No, the Light Body can't do magic and make it so that she has to pay only for the new house by attaching the other money to the mortgage. Nor can she put no money down on the next house, since the downturn of the housing market made it difficult to buy a house without a down payment. But the Light Body can make this woman realize that she must follow the laws of the land she is living in.

The Light Body can clear the woman's aura so she becomes nicer to her employees. The Light Body can motivate her to lose the hundred pounds that she gained while she was drinking and also get her interested in other things besides drinking. And, the Light Body can make this soul see and understand what she is doing wrong and that her way is not going to work. The Light Body can help her stop being so frustrated, as that is what is making huge growths erupt on the skin of her face. These things take time, however.

If you have a friend who is this stubborn and wants to change his or her life but not in the conventional way, then call on that person's Light Body for help.

The realtor told this woman at the settlement table that the debt was paid on her old property at the time of sale and the new house would bring a different debt. She said that the woman would have to provide a down payment because the interest on her type of loan was extremely high. The realtor said that he would help her find the best way to refinance the property so she could then move on. She asked, "Do I have to paint?"

He said, "Yes. It must be beige, because people in this state like beige. And you must clean the carpet and move all of the huge pieces of furniture out to make the place look bigger." The woman was sad because she didn't want to do things in the conventional way. She has the irritation on her skin because she wants to do things her own way. She doesn't want to conform but wants to make up her own rules. She has been thinking these things for years, so the thought-forms that developed in her aura as a result make her rethink things over and over again. She is miserable. When the Light Body breaks the bubble that this woman has been living in while thinking of how to get rid of the condo, the woman might be able to change her thinking. If that happens, then she will see her skin clear up. She might lose some weight and start to see sunshine in her life once again.

When a soul continues to think one thing over and over again, it begins to believe it. This woman's predictions haven't materialized. Several people have told her that the housing market doesn't work the way she thinks it does and that she has to sell her condo and buy a new house another way. She became frustrated and irritated in general and also nasty at work. She is in a vicious spiral, going downward in life, but she could have a wonderful life writing poetry and even making money from it. God always blesses those who do a job for him.

The karmic board, having sent this soul down to earth, sees that she has failed God and herself by being so stubborn. Yet she blames God for her life when it's not God's fault. It's her own thinking that is confusing her. When others tell her the truth, she says, "I don't want to hear this anymore. Don't talk about it again with me!" The realtor showed her how much money she was spending on the interest-only loan and she was in shock. It was thousands of dollars. Instead of getting up and doing something about it, she ran to a winery, bought a case of wine, and drank it in two weeks.

When we in the Octaves see this sort of thing, we begin thinking that we should change out the soul again and see if that helps. We asked several souls who could write, *"Would you like the job to embody and begin to write poetry?"* All those we asked turned down the job because this woman is overweight and has a horrible-looking skin condition. They all said that she was so stubborn that it would take her new soul a couple of years to find itself before beginning to change. So we called on the woman's Light Body one more time to see if we could save this soul. If we can't save this soul on earth, then we will remove her. She can learn what happened to her from the Octaves, go back to school, begin to work in the Octaves again, and regain her strength and belief in God. We will teach her not to be stubborn, and she will learn to work alongside the rest of us. We will bathe her in love and talk to her about what she was facing in life, explaining that she was not successful because her thinking was off, as evidenced by the eruptions on her face.

The woman's college friend who since moved away with her husband will face karma because she knew that this type of loan was not right for her friend. Someone will come along and take her for her money. You are not allowed to cheat another person, smile about it, and then walk away to go count your money and put it in the bank. The stubborn woman realizes that her college friend didn't do right by her. She thought that if her college friend came back to the state, she would help her, but the realtor explained to her, "We are all licensed and must follow the laws that are set up in the state and in the federal government. When selling property, there are things we can do and some things we can never do. You were taken by your friend to get the house sold, and that is a shame. I have seen it time and time again when a friendship is involved and one friend trusted the other, only to realize later that he or she was taken. I am sorry that you had this experience, but if you want me to help you, we need to find out how much you owe on the condo. Then, I believe, we can sell it for [X] amount of dollars since it doesn't have any upgrades. At this point in time, I wouldn't upgrade anything, since you are losing money on it. Sell it as is and you will lose more money; sell it with new paint and remove the big furniture, and we can get a fairly decent price, but it will not pay off the balance. You would have to come to the table with a check to pay off the balance on this piece of property. Then, you can buy your next home."

When the realtor left the condo, the woman was in tears. You see, this soul doesn't want to hear the truth about life. What the realtor discussed is what it takes to sell a house in this woman's home state. It is what all residents of that state must do. If you want to grow and actually make the ascension, then you must face the truth and start on the pathway, knowing what you need to know and working with the negative things, so you can bring your life back into positive balance. A Light Body can change your life, but you must be able to listen to truth. If you need to lose weight, then lose it. If you need to have a softer voice, then practice speaking more softly. If you want to be creative, then take art or singing lessons. A soul must work for everything worth having in this world. If you want to make the ascension, become a Cosmic Being, and never return to earth, then live a life of kindness and love. Think upon God and do godly things for others and you will make it. The negative behaviors that a person exhibits on earth hurt not only that person's soul, but also everyone who encounters that soul. The woman who once was happy is now a fat alcoholic who has horrible skin problems, all because she won't hear truth and doesn't want to do things the conventional way, as the law of the land dictates.

When the instrument wanted to sell her condo, we helped her. She said, "I want to sell it in the springtime." We told her to call the realtor and see what it would go for.

Once the realtor arrived and the two started talking, he said, "You will need to store your big furniture and paint this place beige. You need to pack up all the pictures and knickknacks before we put the condo on the market." He asked, "When will I be able to list it?"

She said, "In three weeks." When he called her, everything was ready to go. He came over and didn't find one thing wrong with the condo. He took pictures and then listed the property for sale. The condo sold in one day. The instrument follows what the law of the land dictates. If it calls for beige paint, then beige it will be. She moved into her new home in the country.

If only the woman whom I have been speaking about would do what she needed to do, then she would be much happier. God and her friends want to see her much happier. Her parents would love to see a change in their daughter. They hope that she eventually marries. But until she changes her mind, until her Light Body reaches her, and until she becomes open to change, she will live very unhappily. Change is the key to success, at times. When you have a loss, cut it loose and move forward. Don't hang onto it. If this woman would cut her losses and move forward with her life, then she would learn much and grow from this experience. She would be able to tell others about her plight and educate them, thereby helping people. Experiences bring wisdom. When you meet a person who is going through the same things you once went through, you have both compassion and wisdom to tell them what they need to do to free them from that experience. And you will have made a lifelong friend.

Chapter Eight

In this book, I have told you some stories about souls on earth whom the instrument doesn't know. I pulled these experiences from the karmic board, which has considered taking other measures when dealing with some of the souls I have mentioned.

However, not too long ago in the Octaves, we would send newly crossed-over souls to school for a few months and tell them what they failed at. We'd send them down to earth in a matter of three or four months unless they were Cosmic Beings returning from a tour of duty on earth. That is what we call it: a tour of duty. We consider it a job. No matter what God asks us to do, we look at it as a job. What you do in your work environment is a job too. If you work hard, then God will bless you, provided that you are not an ascended master. You will be working your way toward becoming an ascended master. In the following year, you become a Cosmic Being and thereafter, remain a Cosmic Being. By the way, just making the ascension puts you at the bottom of the ladder, on the first step. All next steps indicate your gradually increasing level of ascension.

In the Octaves, we used to hear a male soul (Uncle Joe we will call him) call out for a women soul (Aunt Mary) because they knew each other on earth, because he missed her. The Angels would come and comfort him. Aunt Mary was not a very nice person except to her husband of fifty years. Either to her neighbors or people from her past life, when she worked in the church, this gave her the opportunity to be nasty to other souls that were working in the same community church. Looking upon an individual one could not imagine the person's life unless one knew or witnessed the life with that soul to know if they were once nasty or rude or they were a very nice person to all who met that soul. In Aunt Mary's case for instance she could be looked upon as a nice old lady, but she made karma when she was a younger women. When an individual looks at another person on earth; whether it's in church or a grocery store or shopping mall, humans can't gage their spiritual growth by looking upon another human being. In Aunt Mary's case her spiritual development when she was younger was under developed but as she matured she became wiser and her behavior improved and she showed love and kindness to all in her senior years. No human on earth can really see if a person is high or low on the ladder of spiritual development. One could have been a sweet old lady who, when young and pretty, was nasty and hurt others. All that karma comes back to her. And everyone receives that karma in the same way, as the nasty soul who dished it out. So, if Aunt Mary had a habit of telling people off, then she was told off by others. That is a speculative example of how karma comes back to a person. No human on earth can look at another and assess the person's growth on the spiritual ladder.

I now return to the topic of a new crossover. Often, after we sent a person down to earth to start a new life, it was evident four months afterward that he or she hadn't learned to retain a mind-set of thinking on God. As a result, we would send this type of individual to school for twelve to fifteen hours a day to be trained and learn what he or she had needed, but had failed, to do in the previous life. We take the soul back to family or friends and show the individual what these people think about him or her now that he or she has crossed over.

My next story is about two women who lived in different states. The two lived with a husband, were good cooks, were fat and nasty individuals (but were nice to their husbands), loved dogs and other pets, and were nicer to their pets than to their children. Both married when they were young and remained married for more than thirty years. They both developed a form of cancer and died from surgical complications. When they thought they were going to awake from surgery, they left their bodies. They had enough! Most souls do that when they want out of a situation. When they both crossed over, they were in the hospital. We knew they were coming even though they were not supposed to die at that time. Each had said, "I've had enough of life. When I saw an out, I took it." They both had funerals.

One of the women had blonde hair and several dogs. She was married to a Frenchman, to whom she was rude and nasty. She behaved the same way toward women at work sometimes too. This woman attended her own funeral. We always bring souls to their funerals, wanting to show them who loved them. From my point of view, I see that some funeral attendees are nice and others are not so nice. The aura is a dead giveaway of what a person is like on the inside, but humans can't see the aura around a human body. They judge people by their words and actions or how they treat others as well as another.

When we took Blondie, as I will call her, to her funeral, she saw a co-worker standing at the podium reading a poem she had written about the deceased. When the Cosmic Being and Blondie first walked into the funeral home, Blondie said, "I had thought that my co-worker was a nice person? She seemed so happy at work. But now I see that she is another woman who has a horrible aura. What is this all about?"

The Cosmic Being said, "That is what your aura looked like when you were down on earth. You see, you were not a very nice person, either, and so I wanted to show you what the aura of a person who is not nice looks like. Humans on earth can't see the aura, but we can see it from heaven. We then know how to help that person and try to change him or her into someone nicer."

Blondie was in shock, asked, "Why does my husband have his aura that way? It's blank."

The Cosmic Being said, "Because he never loved you."

In tears, she said, "I thought he loved me?"

The Cosmic Being said, "You can see that he is not crying. He is just thinking of what he will do with his life now that you are gone."

Blondie asked, "Why?"

The Cosmic Being said, "Because you were horrible to him and he is glad to see that you have left earth. Now he is seeking a happier life than the one he had with you for thirty years. He is still a young man and can marry a nice woman and be very happy for years to come, never thinking of you again other than to say, 'Glad that it's over!'

"I want to take you to a person who was nice to you and to everyone else so you can see her aura and detect the difference between the life of this soul and that of the woman who is reading poetry and trying to show that she is worth something. She is not worth much to God because she hurt her family by amassing great debt and being nasty to her children. Still, she is up here in front of this group, showing them that she amounted to something. If others knew who she really was and how she really acted, then they would crawl away into a hole. I want you to see what we see from the Octaves. Besides I want you to know how we notice souls on earth and how we give blessings to those who have wonderful auras. To those who don't have wonderful auras, we return their karma immediately.

"When humans form large crowds to watch ball games or concerts, for example, we are there, giving out blessings to some and returning karma to others. It takes us but a few hours to go through the entire audience."

The Cosmic Being then took Blondie to another woman's house. The woman was relaxing and reading a book while playing with her cats. The house was clean and neat, and the woman was happy to be by herself. She prayed before turning out the light and going to sleep. Blondie said, "Oh my. I had no idea that she was that nice. I was jealous of her since she is a good worker and knows her stuff. I didn't want to be shown up by her."

The Cosmic Being said, "That is your karma. You will be nice to everyone in your next life. You will be kind and think upon God." Blondie signed the contract stipulating that she would become a changed soul and do what God wanted her to do. We did a soul exchange and placed her in the USA, in a state where it snows and is cold. She is thirty years old, unmarried, and very pretty—and happier than she has ever been. Nice to everyone she meets, she loves life. So far, this is a success story, but Blondie did go into shock when she saw what the Cosmic Being showed her about her life. She hadn't realized that her husband didn't love her and was very hurt over that bit of news. In fact, after the Cosmic Being took this soul to see what she needed to see, he said, "Let's go and see what your husband is doing now that the funeral is over." They went to her husband's house. He was smiling while getting rid of her clothes and playing music. He was happy for the first time in years. Today, that male soul is remarried. He never says a word about his late wife because he doesn't want anyone to know that he is thrilled that she is gone.

The second woman about whom I will tell you had dark hair and was not much of a worker. She married a man who had a higher-education degree. He made the money for the household, and she came with baggage, which were two beautiful children. The husband, kind, nice, and soft-spoken, adored them. Not long after he married their mother did he realize that he was not in love with her. But he adored those two children, so he stayed in the marriage for thirty years. He felt a little sorry for his wife, who had emotional problems. He talked with her about the childhood experiences that gave rise to her problems.

As life went on, the wife was nasty toward many people. But one thing she could do was cook very well. Everyone loved to come to her house and eat her marvelous food.

When the children moved out, the woman wanted to spruce up the house, but her husband said, "No. We really don't have the money." Later, she was feeling low and decided to go to a doctor. The doctor ran some tests and found that the woman had cancer of the stomach. Sad to know that she would soon leave earth, she cried. Her husband took care of her until the last day, when he sent her to the hospital to die. Both children were there. They walked out of the hospital with dry eyes. Hugging each other, they said, "See you at the funeral."

Their father said, "Come over to the house, see if there is anything you want from your mother's things, and take them." The children did find a few things that they wanted, but there were still no tears in their eyes.

Only a handful of people attended the funeral. They all cried. One asked, "How are the children taking their mother's death?"

The husband said, "I think they are in shock and it will hit them when they are home and see that she is finally gone."

After the funeral, everyone went out to eat. They talked about the deceased, saying that she could be either a miserable or a funny person to be around.

Once the husband got home, he called his mother in Latin America and said, "I need to come see you and talk to you." He took a flight there. While he was hugging his mother after saying hello, she asked, "Where is your wife Susan?"

He said, "Well, she passed away." His mother was in shock. "I didn't want to burden you with her death," he said.

After returning from Latin America, he took a month off from work to adjust to his wife's death, but still no tears.

We took the wife to see her husband. He was walking down the street, so happy that he could almost skip. Every day that passed found him happier. His wife, in shock, was angry! The Cosmic Being asked, "Why are you getting mad?"

She said, "Because he is happy and I am dead."

The Cosmic Being said, "He never loved you. You are just finding that out now. You see his aura? That is what happiness looks like to us. From this level of heaven, we see who is happy, who is sad, who is nasty, and who is mean. Your aura looked like that of the woman sitting on the bench. She is nasty and mean to others. Your husband couldn't love you, given your behavior. No one in your family loved you; they tolerated you. And that is what I wanted to show you."

The woman was so upset that she stopped talking to the Cosmic Being. He took her to see her family, all her brothers and sisters. Not a one of them thought twice about her departure from this life. They were watching TV, eating dinner out, or playing on the computer as they would if it were any other day. The woman was upset and crying. The Cosmic Being said, "You will be nice to everyone in your next life. You will be charming and kind to those you meet all the days of your life. And you will believe in and love God."

After having her attend school for three months, we pushed this soul down into a body left over from a soul exchange. We see where she has improved, but she is not a success story as of yet. We are watching this woman's soul. If things don't change, then we will move her out, put a young girl in that body, and let that girl have a happy life. We will no longer waste God's time by trying to make a soul do things that it is ready to do. It is hard for some souls to believe in God. Being kind to others and loving their fellows is hard for these souls, so we subject them to more training. Those in the Octaves waiting to be rewarded with a body will be rewarded when we see souls such as this one not making significant efforts to change. We will change out this woman and then keep her in the Octaves to work with her. We will give her body to someone deserving who will serve God and help mankind. We want all souls to work for God. If they won't, then we have plenty others who are ready for a tour of duty on earth. These souls will love performing that duty because they deserve it and have passed the test of being kind and loving toward their fellows while working their hearts out for mankind in the Octaves. We are tired of nasty souls. **We never send a soul down to earth to hurt another being. That is not our style, and it's surely not God's style.** Nasty souls are self-willed. We tell them to straighten up, but they are willful and do not. We will change them out, and then they will be taught. They will have to prove to us that they are worthy of having a body on earth. We have done over two thousand soul exchanges in the last month and continue to do more. When we change out a soul, we are sure that the new one is loving and kind; loves God; and will be a blessing on earth to everyone he or she meets.

Those who are not blessings will have a soul exchange and then learn in the Octaves. We hope that in five years the world will have a better feeling and vibration to it, that there will be fewer wars on earth and more happiness and love. We hope that all people will love each other and embrace the differences that people from each culture have to offer. **Respect, respect, respect and love is the key to making the ascension.** When you have those ingredients, God inhabits your heart. When you love God, you also love your fellows and wouldn't dream of hurting them.

Chapter Nine

In the past, we did things differently in the Octaves. We found that some things worked and other things had to be changed. Some of the results we saw were not what we ultimately wanted. About four years ago, before we had a planet that was six hours away by Space Ship. We would send all the new crossovers to a different planet. There, they underwent a reaping process before going on to training and then to the karmic board, the last stop in the process of accepting a new body.

During the reaping process, all souls' memories of past lives were blanked out because, at the time, we felt that a blank slate was best for a soul when it resumed the tests on earth after beginning a new life. As we watched souls develop on earth, we noticed that the memory-wiping-out-process had little effect, whether a soul remembered his past lives or didn't remember they seemed to go about their life. Exceptional souls or any souls didn't remember their past lives; and no Cosmic Beings remembered that they were Cosmic Beings. Now, we have opened up the channels for all Cosmic Beings so that they can remember what or who they are. We are hoping that with the title of Cosmic Being, they will recall how to act and remember that they have a responsibility to God to act godly in all areas of their lives. Just like a company's vice president is expected to behave according to company rules regarding business conduct and must exhibit the utmost honesty when conducting business deals, we expect our Cosmic Beings to behave according to our rules. Sometimes, although it's rare,

Cosmic Beings fail. In that case, we send them back down to earth to work off the karma.

We no longer put souls through the reaping process because it is unnecessary. We moved all the souls from the planet we formerly used back to the Earth. These souls now train all new crossovers. In the Octaves, we train all the children after they have had a soul exchange because they were failing life. Their parents, who are Cosmic Beings, ask them to come home so they can teach them how to act on earth, hoping that they will make the ascension. If the Cosmic Beings feel that the children are doing what they are supposed to do, then we leave the children on earth. Those children who are not doing well and whose behavior hasn't changed, even after their parents have wakened them at night and talked to them for months, off and on, are pulled from earth, at which point we do a soul exchange, which takes about twenty minutes. Afterward, the children awake and wonder *where am I?* Of course, they are sad to have been pulled from earth and told that they can't continue with their destructive behavior, hurt others, or do what they want to do: not believe in God.

We monitor these souls, even if they are in their forties or fifties, as if they were very young children because they failed the test on earth and did not grasp what they were supposed to learn. While these souls have parents on earth who love them, they find out that their real parents are in the Octaves, which shocks them, as most humans on earth don't realize that they have different parents in the heavenly world. The karmic board picks parents for a young soul, usually a couple who promise God and the karmic board that they will raise the child a certain way, provide a godly atmosphere, and support the child in all his or her endeavors. The parents sign a contract to this effect before being excused by the karmic board.

When a body is ready, the karmic board calls the child souls. They come. Sometimes, the body is used for a soul exchange. Other times, the bodies belong to parents who were being raised on earth and then had children to raise, doing what God wanted them to do for those children.

On earth, all across the globe, many companies and government agencies need to implement changes but are reluctant to do so. The employees ask, "Why can't upper management see what changes need to be made when it's so obvious to everyone else?" In our particular case, when we were making changes, we hadn't started looking at the problem until the evil ones began fighting with us. For days at a time, we had to stop what we were doing for mankind. When we came back to deal with our own workload, we noticed that the souls that had crossed over were not improving. After all of the training and education, they missed connecting the dots in their lives and even failed small tests. At that point, we asked, "What are we doing? This is a waste of precious time.

Let's block their memories from here on out." We did that, but we still send all souls to training to remind them about God and being kind when they enter bodies. We realized that they sometimes did not listen during the training sessions. They were interested in leaving the Octaves and returning to earth, which posed a problem because they were still willful souls. So now we do many soul exchanges to pull them from earth. When a soul exchange is done, it takes about two years before we see the new soul take over and start to change the life it entered. Sometimes, a newly incarnated soul fails. We either change it out again or else remove that soul from earth and set it straight about why we pulled it from earth, mentioning how it had failed and asking, "Why didn't you do what you were supposed to do in that life?" Most of the recently exchanged souls are improving. We have added more Cosmic Beings to the mix of un-ascended souls on earth, making a better balance. In an attempt to give all souls a chance on earth, we sometimes move a soul from one body to a different one in another country. The reason for this is that some cultures on earth have strict rules for women. We move some female souls who are loose to a culture where promiscuity is prohibited. These souls seem to do well in a more disciplined culture. When some cross over, they realize that they were on earth for more than a hundred years.

Into newly vacated fifty-year-old bodies, we put Cosmic Beings or young souls so they live a disciplined life rather than being loose with their morals. Sometimes, I look at souls when they make changes to their lives and wonder, *Are they connecting the dots?* No, they were pulled from their bodies because they couldn't connect the dots. The cosmic Beings with whom we did soul exchanges on who finished out those lives they can connect the dots. The removed souls are sent to live in a more disciplined culture, where they must toe the line.

We also match skill sets. If a soul doesn't have many skills, then we put a different one into its previous body to make a match. Let's say that we want to change out a person who has a beautiful voice and is famous on earth. We would replace her soul with one that has sung before and can still sing. A writer has to be replaced by another writer. It is the same way for a doctor. We have exchanged doctor souls before because some of them wanted to come home. We take them from earth as a soul exchange. The family and friends left behind don't notice any change at first, as the changes appear subtly. One has to be aware enough to see them.

In certain rare situations, we send to earth a Cosmic Being or BEING who has come to help us. Then, after these souls travel back to their planets, they take a body and offer to help the individuals to whom they are married learn about love. They have children; some of them adopt. Say that one such adopted child has special needs. He or she is there to teach the mother, a woman soul, about unconditional love. The woman soul must love that child, who is a Cosmic Being, even though the child is not perfect. Sometimes, the woman becomes unhappy about having adopted the child, while the husband, a BEING, adores the child. The other two children love their adopted brother and everyone gets along. The unhappy mother begins to complain because it takes her longer to get things done for the special-needs child. She becomes impatient with him. Soon, the father sees this and realizes, after a year, that the woman soul will not learn that she is to love this special-needs child. She wants the child to be removed from the home or else she will leave the family. So, the man soul comes up to the karmic board and says, "I need to shorten my stay, and these are the reasons." He explains that the woman will not learn from the child whom he adores and that she wants to move him to another home. She wishes to keep the two children to whom she gave birth. The husband is distraught, as he loves the child and doesn't want to give him up, but his wife is forcing the issue. He appears very upset to the karmic board and asks if his tour of duty with this woman can be over.

We see several cases like this one at the karmic board, where the souls will not learn or are forced to do things they don't want to do and so they want to leave the situation. In this case, the Cosmic Being husband would no longer love his wife if he had to give up the child they adopted. The karmic board pulled him from earth and did a soul exchange for him. The child was moved to another family and is now very happy, as he was happy with his other family. The two other children are adjusting. This story will end with everyone happy. But in the woman soul's next life, she will have special-needs children to take care of and will learn to love and accept them. She made karma because she did not do what God wanted her to do in this lifetime. The whole structure of this family was set up for this one woman soul to learn to love unconditionally.

As we continue to provide stories from the Karmic Board about souls and the different experiences each one experienced. We are trying to show the reader different scenarios of how souls upon this earth have experiences and the reader is supposed to use these stories in their life to reflect and learn from them. We have many thousands of stories to present to the reader obviously we can't use all of them. As a Light Body, I wanted to use stories of souls that would relate to the current reader today. In this next story about a soul I explain about cheating and how God deals with this type of behavior.

One man soul married for the second time in his life. At first, he was happy with his second wife. After he first met her, he had an affair with her while still married to his first wife? Cheating is against God's laws, but, still, this soul acquired a new spouse because he was unhappy with his first wife, with whom he had two children. The two boys are now raised. The second wife is good-looking, prettier than the first wife. She, a person from a different country and with a foreign accent, was used to shopping at the finest stores since her ex-husband was wealthy. For her, spending four hundred dollars on a pair of shoes was normal. Her bed-sheets cost thousands of dollars. This impressed the male soul when he first met her. She was decked out from head to toe. Her husband kicked her out of the house and then flew home to his country. She now had no place to live since she had no job and had never worked for a living. The male soul, with whom she was smitten, said, "Move in with me." They started out in an apartment and eventually bought a house in an up-and-coming area where the houses were very expensive. Her family had left her with plenty of money, so she could afford this house after her father had passed away; he had willed a trust to the daughter.

The male soul was supposed to learn to be honest in that lifetime but was failing. Both he and his second wife told stories about their lives, but that is just what they were *stories*. Both of them were dishonest. At the time, though, they were in love and thrilled to be with each other.

When the new house was built, the man was working at his low-paying job and stealing from his customers. Realizing that it was expensive to maintain his wife and not wanting to lose her, he hustled to make more sales and, therefore, more money. His wife, beginning to shop overseas, spent $20,000 to fill the house with luxury items she loved. Since she hadn't taken much from her ex-husband, she now bought brand new things! When the bills came in, her husband was working six or seven days a week. She was out buying very expensive sheets for the bed and ordering golf shoes from Italy. Life was moving forward. The bill to paint the house, which included scrollwork on the walls, was over $5,000. The man was still happy but saw that he couldn't keep up with the bills. The credit cards presented him with mounting debt.

After ten years of marriage, his business went flat during the economic downturn. Some people in the United States lost their houses and moved elsewhere in the country in search of better jobs. The country was in turmoil, the banking sector was in trouble, and the housing market had collapsed. The male soul, frustrated and unhappy, said, "This is not a life that I can take anymore. I need to leave earth." We called him up to the karmic board and asked him what happened? He said, "I don't like what I turned out to be in this life. My family doesn't like me, and I can't stand my wife. She spends so much money that I am losing my house. She refuses to work. Her mother will not lend us the money to keep the house. I am being foreclosed on since I can't make the mortgage payments." He cried. "I was supposed to learn to be honest. I need to make enough money to accommodate her spending habits. We are arguing. I tell her that I don't have the money coming in as I once had, but she doesn't seem to care. She is spending two hundred dollars a week on food. It's all adding up to where I am drowning."

As we listened to him, we saw that this soul had gotten in over his head. He was frustrated and crying, knowing that he was failing. He couldn't keep up with his wife's needs and desires, so we changed him out as a soul exchange. That was more than five years ago. The woman soul didn't see the changes until she had to move out of their huge half-million-dollar home. She lived for a short while in a very nice rental. Once the man's soul exchange took effect, we discovered that the new soul in his body was much stronger. The new soul stopped the wife from spending money the couple didn't have. She ultimately went to live with her mother in her native country. The original male soul is now living with a loving family, as he was put into a five-year-old body. Prior to the soul exchange, the male soul was in his sixties. He will live approximately a hundred and twenty years on earth and have two lives. The woman soul, having noticed changes in her husband, said to him when she was leaving, "I don't know you anymore." And to some extent, that was true, given the soul exchange. The new male soul in this body is doing fine. He is dating a nice woman. They are planning to live together but have not made the move as of yet. He has learned not to cheat innocent people and also to live within his means.

The male soul and his second wife created karma together by cheating on their respective spouses. Those types of relationships rarely last because of the way in which the two individuals entered the relationship. Wait until the person whom you like and are interested in untangles him - or herself from any present relationship before starting your own relationship with that person. This type of relationship is doomed most of the time. The male soul realizes these things now, after almost twenty years. He has thought much about his life and has grown from this experience. This was a successful soul exchange. The five-year-old boy is now in a loving home and attends church on Sundays with his family. His family adores him and teaches him how to be honest and kind to all human beings on earth. In his last life, he was neither kind nor honest with his family or his wives. He frequently cheated on his first wife and had a mistress for over ten years. He acquired karma by behaving that way, but, at this time, he is moving forward with his life as a nice, young soul who is growing in God. The wife who moved in with her mother has not learned much about life except how to spend her mother's money. When her mother crosses over, the woman soul will learn about managing finances, being honest, loving others, and learning how to depend on God. The water well of her mother's money is running dry in a country where things are very expensive to buy.

As we evolve during our battles with the evil ones, we change out a lot of willful, rude, nasty, or evil souls on earth. They need to be retrained and learn why they were sent to earth in the first place. If we can't change them out, then we update their profiles and remove them from earth when they become sick. That is usually our last resort. We try and try over and over again to make souls realize what they need to change and begin to do right for God. All souls on earth have the chance to change the positions they are in by leaving their bodies at night, coming up to the karmic board, and asking for a change. Sometimes, change is the best thing for a soul.

Reader, if your situation is not a particularly a nice one and you would like to make a change to believe more in God by being presented with the right conditions, then come to the karmic board and be heard. A group of men and women Cosmic Beings sit on this board, which meets in a theater-like room where the panel is in front of you. You stand in line and wait your turn to voice your concerns about your life. Nightly, thousands of souls come up to be heard. When you go to sleep at night, tell your Light Body to take you up to the karmic board so you can voice your opinion about your life on earth. Your Light Body will bring you up. Within a few months, you will either be in another body or back in the Octaves. With a soul exchange, you can start all over again and deal with your particular issue. Or, perhaps, you have no issues but see that your life is not producing any inner growth. Many souls, tired of living on earth, feel this way. At this time, we exchange their souls. Also, we exchange souls for those who are very high souls on earth and have accomplished much in their lives. Because they are so highly valued, we in the Octaves see no sense in their dusting the living room furniture or mopping the floors. We have more important things for them to do. When we do soul exchanges for them, we match their skills, if they have cultivated any on earth, and put into the body a soul that will finish up that life by doing mundane things. The new soul can work out any small issues. We have seen two souls achieve their goals in this way. The high soul is valued in the Octaves and can help us battle the evil ones, and the newly exchanged soul can finish out the other soul's life projects.

When we do this type of soul exchange, each soul, the old and the new, must have the same skill set, for instance, singing, typing, writing, creating art, acting, or dancing. Skills required for certain professions—in science, medicine, or law, for example—must match up. We must be cautious when making soul exchanges because we sometimes exchange government officials and heads of state.

When some souls cross over, they find it difficult to detach from materialism. In the Octaves, we have a ranking system, as I explained before. The higher you are, the more jewels, including diamonds, you can wear on your clothes. The less light you have, the plainer your raiment and robes. Materialism is a problem for most of the souls that cross over. Some may have been prominent people on earth who have no wisdom in their spiritual bodies. They are very earthly, as we say, believing that money gets a person everything, as is the case on earth. But a soul needs wisdom up here, as wisdom translates to light. The light we have shines within our bodies. We can either display or hide it, but, in any event, we control it. For the most part, Octaves' lights show.

When a female soul who didn't work and was married to a rich man crosses over, she feels that she is rich too because she was married to a rich man. Well, when she was accustomed to buying expensive things and having people wait on her, she was adept at decorating, shopping, gardening, or going to lunch with her girlfriends. This does not represent a life of wisdom. Rather, it is a life that the soul earned by doing something nice for others at one time. At times, we give souls a lifetime "off." What this means is that they can have a happy life and not be expected to work specifically on a fault or work to gain wisdom, or work on their karma.

Some souls burn out and can no longer endure a life on earth. When we see that they failed in their past lives, we give them a life off to see if they will work on themselves without having to sign a contract between them and the karmic board, as if it was mandatory to gain wisdom, learn to be kind and love nature and animals, and help their fellow souls on earth. Unfortunately, most of these souls never learn much. Contrary to popular belief, they are usually not nice people and think they are better than others on earth. They have a hard time adjusting in the next life when we say, "Now you must go back and learn to love and work again, rather than being married to a rich man [or woman] and being taken care of. Your previous life was for you to rest on earth and do what you wanted to do." The soul either uses that time to help others because he or she can afford it or else wastes that lifetime; most of the time, these souls waste the lifetime off. When they cross over wearing a plain dress, they want a diamond dress and become depressed for some time because they were accustomed to wearing designer labels. They are not allowed to wear heavenly designer labels, which are jeweled or diamond dresses for women or robes for men. We send them to training to gain the wisdom they need. We illuminate what they thought about in their last lives and compare the differences. If they have an entitlement problem, then they begin working on it.

All of us in the heavenly realm have met souls who think they are better than other souls because they lived in a certain place on earth, owned a huge house, or drove an expensive luxury car. These souls come to realize the shocking difference between living in the Octaves and on earth. On earth, one can be selfish, rude, and nasty and pretend to be better than others. While one may exhibit these horrible traits on earth, these things don't help anyone in the heavenly world. If you have those traits when you cross over, you are sent to training to develop a conscience and learn how to think more spiritually. On earth, when you see other souls on the street or at a concert, for example, don't make derogatory statements about them. You have no idea who those people are or what they are working on during that lifetime.

Sometimes, a new crossover asks about a person with whom he or she was friends on earth, wanting to rekindle that friendship. When the old friends meet again, sometimes it's a shock to learn that one friend had more money and so thought that he was higher than his friend, who lived in a modest house, drove an average car, and only took his family to vacation at the river, since that was what he could afford. His friend, however, flew from the United States to Europe. A soul who thinks of him-or herself as superior to others is something we see on a daily basis in the Octaves. We have a team of Cosmic Beings who work with crossed-over souls that had a certain idea about heaven. These souls are in shock when they find that the Octaves are run like a civilization with plenty of rules. We train those souls and teach them to have a change in attitude. In their minds, they were glorious and expected to rock everyone's world when they arrived in the Octaves. It is a huge shock when they cross over and this doesn't happen.

The wisdom that you carry is the wisdom that shines within you like a flashlight. The Queen of Queens, when she comes to talk to us, turns down her light. She carries so much light that it can burn souls. She realizes this. Very kind, she wants everyone to have much light and grow. The more light and Cosmic Beings on earth, the more apt we are to reach a state of peace. When we reach that state of peace, many things will change on earth. People will not feel the need to build bombs or weapons of mass destruction. Some souls on earth think that world peace would be great. We agree. This is what we are working on in our arena. But when world peace arrives, life on earth will change in the work environment for those employed in the security area of our country. At this time, I ask you to call on your Light Body and express your concerns. Let your Light Body begin to work on your life and change what needs to be changed or enhance what needs to be enhanced so you can reach your goal for this lifetime, pass the initiations, and make the ascension. May you be blessed in the days to come as you make a new journey and talk to your Light Body.

Made in the USA
San Bernardino, CA
09 November 2016